The Other Side of Tourism demonstrates that
hot weather, white beaches, rum punch and ot
ures are found in the personali

KDP Amazon, Paperback Edition, 2021

Copyright © 1993 by Myrna Loy

A Cataloguing in Publication (CIP) catalogue record for this book is available from the British Library.

ISBN: 9798599835363

This Second Edition is published and printed in the United Kingdom, by KDP Amazon, an imprint of independently published.

Originally published in paperback in the United Kingdom by Art's Own Gallery, an imprint of self-publisher, in 2004.

Photography and Poetry by Myrna Loy

Every effort has been made to ensure the accuracy of this text at the time of going to press. The Publisher would be grateful for notification of errors or omissions.

ACKNOWLEDGEMENTS

Thanks first, to the Creator in whom ALL things are possible; to Jamaica, the perpetual home of my parents; to the Jamaican language without which this book could not be written; to my parents, daughters, friends, relations and work colleagues who were a constant source of support and motivation.

I would also like to mention my Jamaican sisters who gave me insight into the Jamaican female mentality, and to my Jamaican brothers for giving me insight into the Jamaican male.

To www.jamaicans.com who helped promote the book through 'sneak previews' on their website. To everyone who has supported me and helped promote the book directly and indirectly, the list is endless – THANK YOU ALL.

CONTENTS PAGE

INTRODUCTION

Being born in England of Jamaican parents, I should have had the best of both worlds, but I used to get confused about by my identity because my mother would belittle the Jamaican side of it. She believed everything British had to be better, so she would chastise me when I tried to emulate her dialect as if she was ashamed of it; but there was something about the Jamaican language that enthused me.

My mother was always instilling in me its mediocrity, so I deliberately and defiantly opposed her by mimicking uncles and aunts who came to visit, and by reinforcing the culture in my day-to-day language, in my writings, and through my JamaicArt painting series.

I wanted to transfer this precious culture beyond my generation. I wanted to tell my mother that by denouncing her language she was admonishing her heritage, but I had a traditional mother who might have taken umbrage, so I taught my children to embrace the culture so that they could carry on the tradition.

English is the language normally spoken in Jamaica but patois was invented to facilitate communication between voluntary and involuntary migrants, so to reject its usage because we are led to believe it is a substandard language used by illiterate people, is an insult.

I mention this because I have written the book in a bi-lingual format (code-switching) to reinforce my struggle to adapt to the culture, and give credence to both identities. Besides the fact, it is the language Black Britons, like myself, relate to.

The patois in this book has not been standardised, and I must add that it is not my intention to ridicule the language in anyway, but simply to express an interaction.   Nor have I resorted to name-calling, as the emotions within tell the story.

It could be argued that I should accept my identity as British. After all I was born in Britain, educated in a British institution, raised by British standards, therefore why the confusion? Why make a mountain out of a molehill and create a need to research a seemingly obvious phenomenon one might ask?

For me, it has to do with reconciling my feelings of self-respect versus isolation. It has to do with finding all the pieces to the puzzle and sorting them out so that they fit together in a cohesive fashion. It had to do with reconciling painful feelings of alienation and social exclusion, which I have experienced in being called a nigger, an immigrant, or an ethnic minority. Similarly, in Jamaica, it was alienating to be called "a foreigner" and "a tooriss", the implication being: "you are not one of us". These factors led me to question where do I belong? Where is my place and, more importantly, where is my home?

So what has all this got to do with Tourism?   Tourism is "the practice of travelling for recreation or culture". This book shares both the recreational and cultural facets of Jamaica, written from the perspective of a Black-British 'tourist' in Jamaica.

The other side of tourism, for me, was travelling to Jamaica with the mindset that because it was the home of my parents, and because of my familiarity with the dialect, food and traditions, I felt I qualified to be acknowledged as Jamaican, but I wasn't, because I wasn't born there.

Spending two weeks in Jamaica was an exhilarating and enlightening experience. Definitely, not long enough to make an accurate assessment, but long enough to make a value judgement, and interesting enough to share my experience with others.

This book will, I hope, enable Black Britons, or anyone else for that matter, to be aware of how Jamaican parenting may have impacted the way some of us view Jamaicans; to understand the idiosyncrasies of the Jamaican culture, and to help us realise that our perception of the culture is just that — nothing personal.

"Negated Identity"
© 2003 by Myrna Loy

Me love de culture, me speak de patois,
h'an yet dem seh me no come fram rown' yah..
Dem call me a touriss h'an a foreigna,
Dem laugh h'an call me h'imitator.
But me jus waan dem fe h'ackept me in Jamaica,
Not as a 'tooriss' but a native sistah!
Being British has its advantages
I don't need a visa to go to a lot of places
I am among a melting pot of different races
Thus, my identity has a lot of different faces
But British and Jamaican have their own spaces
So I am not quite sure where my place is!
I don't understand the differentiation,
When we are all a part of God's ONE nation.

HOW IT ALL STARTED

Retaliation, spite, spontaneity, impetuosity, call it whatever you will, but I decided to go to Jamaica alone, and I would not repeat the experience because the faces of the local people told me that it was not proper, a single woman on the loose—what could she possibly want except our men, our husbands?

My two sisters and I had planned a vacation in Florida, so I had reserved my vacation days to accommodate this. However, at the last minute they both changed their minds for different reasons. They started to make proposals for alternative places to spend a holiday, nothing definite, just: "I was thinking of going to... or maybe we'll end up at... I've never been to... we have to find somewhere to go..." suggestions and ideas, nothing conclusive. This was not the kind of holiday I had been planning for. I had been so excited; I had never been to Florida before, and I would be vacationing with women after my own heart. I had been looking forward to this for weeks, and then, as I was trying to confirm dates and meeting places, I sensed indecision and abandonment of the idea. I didn't really want to go by myself, but I felt I had little choice, and besides, past experience had shown me that to have company would only impose limitations, whether real or implied.

I paid for a package deal (no food or tours included) just hotel room, flight and transportation to and from the airport—two weeks in Montego Bay for US$300. The flight was smooth.

Contrary to what they show in the movies, the femme fatale was not being wooed by a super-looking stud. The man who sat beside me continually apologised for belching. I accepted the blue flannel-type blanket, compliments of Shrouder Airlines and covered my head with it, attempting to minimize the discomfort, but to no avail... intrepidity seeped persistently into my ear lobes.

The plane arrived on schedule in Miami, and the transfer to the connecting plane was straightforward.

JAMAICA, A NEW CULTURE

I had an early flight, arriving in Jamaica about lunch time.

"Taxi, miss—Taxi, ma'am—Hey, miss, yuh waan a taxi?" Distorted mouths and expressions, moulded in black shiny faces, spouted from all directions, competing against each other for a fare. Outstretched palms, ready to snatch reluctant suitcases from rivals. I followed my nose, which didn't have any sense of direction and sighed with relief on seeing 'Jamdung Tourline', the agency responsible for transporting me to the hotel.

I took out my transportation ticket and waited (there was one person in front of me). He left shortly afterwards. I tarried patiently while the representatives engaged themselves in unofficial chatter and un-befitting bouts of laughter.

The polite British culture took over. Most Brits are diplomatic, during frustration, we will not jump up and make a noise. So I tried to drop a hint, by intermittently glancing at my watch, hoping to draw their attention to the fact that I required attention.

It took them 10 minutes to resume composure and ask for my vacation documents. They instructed me to fill out a couple of forms and once I had completed them, one of the representatives said: "Wait, right here... someone in a blue suit will soon come tek yu to de 'otel".

I lingered. Twenty minutes passed. I crouched uncomfortably on my luggage, and then stood up displaying my presence and agitation with tacit composure.

I saw plenty of men attired in blue suits; so, desperately seeking acknowledgement from the agents as to whether any of them could be my driver, I strained in their direction. Involved in indecorous liaison, they ignored me. I approached the desk:

"How long do I have to wait?" I asked. I noticed the Jamaican influence was kicking in.

"im soon come, im soon come" she said in an effort to be helpful.

"never see come see" I mumbled under my breath.

After about ten minutes I heard:

"See im deh," she shouted jubilantly, pointing to a man in a brown overall.

"But I thought you said my driver would be wearing a blue suit?"

"It don't matter, a yu driver dis"

I stood there puzzled. I stretched my neck out to see if there were any identifying marks on the vehicle... "Jamdung-Tourline Bus Service" was ineptly scrawled on a piece of paper in black felt tip and stuck on the inside window of the bus with tape. I shrugged my shoulders, picked up my hand luggage and walked towards the bus.

A rather plump lady approached me in a blue uniform. She was clutching some papers, and had a purse attached to a waist with a piece of blue ribbon. I could tell by the way she pointed her foot out, that she was proud of her shoes. Someone must have sent them to her from foreign. They looked like leather, they had a bar going across with a large buckle.

"My name is Genevieve - me a come wid yu.." she said beaming. She had a Jamdung Tourline label, so I assumed she was a representative doing her job. I didn't answer.

".. me haf fe talk to yu... Mek sure yu meet me in the lobby at 4 o'clock, o.k? It is very important" she instructed.

I always had reservations about people who wanted to talk about something 'later' when the opportunity presented itself there and then. Why the delay? It automatically created an atmosphere of foreboding.
She bungled herself in the front seat and I kept a suspicious eye on my luggage.

"No-one else for this hotel?" I asked wondering if it was indicative of its bad reputation.

"No, not until tomarrow" she replied, curbing her lingo.

I kept silent and looked out of the window.

"It's only five minutes fram de airport.." she offered, as if, after waiting so long it really mattered.

I don't know why I felt so uptight. Well I do know. I sensed no commitment or obligation from the people I had interacted with so far – just nonchalance -, total disrespect for time and inattention to details. My eyes peeled the window of the bus... dusky hills in the background; large stretches of land; goats grazing; a young boy walking barefoot, a man riding a scooter, two youths conversing, (it was a man's world).

We stopped. I was ready to get out when she told me: "is me one a get off here yu know... yu still 'ave a little way to go".

She had previously told me that she was accompanying me (implying that she was procuring my safe arrival to the hotel) when it was just an excuse to use the transportation I had paid for to get a free lift to her destination.

I re-seated myself

"Don't feget... 4 o'clock!" she repeated, through the window, with warped rhetoric.

What was this 4.o'clock business? I just wanted to go into the hotel and lie down. The whole point of me leaving America to come to Jamaica was that I didn't want to be bothered with time. I wanted to do things at my own pace... in my own space... in my own time. I felt she was inflicting restrictions, and I was allowing her to do so. 4 o'clock?! The way I felt, she could wait in the lobby all night for all cared. It was 2.15 in the afternoon. Almost two and a half hours to get to a hotel that was meant to be five minutes away!

"YU ROOM NO READY YET"

The driver put my suitcases down on the lobby floor and stood loitering.

I disliked the way he stood there obviously waiting for compensation when it was clearly written in the contract that all service charges to and from the airport, were included. I also resented the fact that people like him were usually successful in appealing to the softer side of my nature. I gave him a US dollar and went inside.

"Yu room no ready yet" the receptionist said.

"When will it be ready" I asked, exasperated.

Not answering my question she said:

"The management offers a complimentary drink, what would you like, Rum Punch or Fruit Punch?"

"I'll take the Rum Punch, thank you". I needed to quench my thirst, after so much of my vacation time had been wasted.

"By the time you finish your drink your room will be ready" she said smiling.

(She obviously underestimated my ability to consume quickly - it was down the hatch in two seconds flat). Concealing her repugnance, she said:

"Would you like to go and sit over there, ma'am?", she said, pointing to some wicker chairs decorated with floral cushions, in a dimly lit corner next to the entrance of the restaurant. I would be out of eyesight, and so she would not be constantly reminded of my irritation. "Maybe you would like something to eat?"

I walked over to the large menu propped up against a divider.

Ackee and Saltfish US$5.00? Why were they quoting in US Dollars when we were in Jamaica? All the prices were quoted in US dollars. I went and sat down on the soft floral cushions, and decided not to order anything – I was not going to be ripped off!

ROOM SERVICE

I sat around for about forty-five minutes, unable to settle down. In half an hour I was supposed to meet that woman, what was her name? "Genevieve".

I was directed to my room by a foolish-grinning individual who must have thought that he'd struck lucky, me being single, and him being my first encounter.

"My name is Tyrone!" he volunteered proudly.

"Really?" I said, without exchanging my name.

He put down the one suitcase I had brought with me, and proceeded towards the television.

"Yu have cable television, but there is no remote control", he explained with a professional spirit.

He approached the air-conditioner.

"Yu 'ave air-conditioning, too, yu wan' me fe tun it on?" raising his eyebrow as if to signify that he had the ability to please me.

I nodded. He left it off.

"Room service is me, extension 349". His mouth widened as he beamed with anticipation, exposing missing teeth at the back and disclosing what little was left in the front—whittled discoloured protrusions.

"I won't be needing room service, thank you" I assured him.

I looked down at his shoes... shoes told me about the man. He failed miserably. Someone much larger had obviously donated the dust-covered shoes to him, since his feet leaned indeterminably inside them. Wanting to get him out of my sight as quickly as possible, I begrudgingly gave him 1 x US dollar. [24 Jamaican dollar is a whole heap of money—it can buy him one soda if him lucky with change left.]

I put down my things. The hotel was situated right next to the renowned Seagull Seafood Restaurant. 'The Seagull' had a good reputation, so I was happy that it was so close.

I looked around the hotel room. I was not impressed. Someone had practiced a make-shift plastering job on the ceiling; the carpet had stains on it; on examining the sheets they had tears and holes in them, but my consistent evaluation, despite its seemingly unkempt appearance, was that everything was clean.

I turned on the television...nothing interesting - I switched it off. I turned on the air-conditioner, it sounded like frenzied rats hurling their constipated stools at each other, but missing every time, but most importantly, the air-conditioner did the job, the cool air greeted me in a cordial manner.

I went out onto the veranda and watched the ocean seduce the naked beach with envy. In out - in out ... it thrusted forward against the bank and then retreated into itself in easy gliding motion.

A woman carrying a large basket of fruit and vegetables on her head interrupted my observations. Innovative, I thought. I raced to my bag for the camera, but then realised it was not loaded with film. By the time I had put the film in, and fumbled with the instrument, the lady was out of focus. I would be prepared next time I thought, but opportunity knocks but once.

I could see a beach from my window, a counterfeit, designed to fulfil the promise advertised in the brochure of a 'view overlooking the beach'. At night, the imitation was obscured by the evening mist and enhanced by the new moon; it looked beautiful. No one, except those walking barefoot, would realise that the light brown coloured soil was dried grass and not soft sand. The large white rocks, caressing each other, leashed the waters, separating one beach from the other. I went back into the hotel room and took my clothes out of the suitcase to hang them up. I noticed that the hotel had provided deformed wire triangles for this purpose. It was just as well I had brought my own.

JAMDUNG-TOURLINE

The phone rang, I picked it up eagerly. It was the receptionist, informing me that 'Genevieve' (the Jamdung Tourline Rep) was waiting for me in the reception area. I was disappointed, but decided that I would find out what was so important.

When I passed the receptionist, she intercepted me and said:

"I forgot to tell you that you have to put down US$100 as security deposit against incidentals such as the phone, the towels, food, etc. [I resolved that it would be good to have some money left when the vacation was over].

"You will also need a security box for your passport and your money as we are not responsible for items lost in rooms, which will be US$20". I gave her the US$100 and she put it in an envelope and I asked for a receipt. She gave me the key for the security box and told me that if I lost it I would lose the security box deposit of US$10. I took my keys (she didn't give me a receipt for the money) and approached Genevieve who looked pleased to see me.

"Well, how 'ave yu been finding it so far?"
"I haven't been here long enough - it is hard to tell, but it's O.K."

"'ave yu visited Jamaica before?"

"Yes, this is my third time"

"But you are not Jamaican?"

"No, my parents are"

[What was she getting at?]
"Well, I am here to provide yu with information about the area (she

continued, pronouncing each word with forced eloquence).

There is a supermarket down the road, if yu need to buy some rum, or if yu want to buy postcards." [That is handy to know]

"Opposite the supermarket, there is a post office where yu can buy yuh stamps." [Hmmm, maybe it wasn't such a waste of time].

"There are three beaches, the Howard Fletcher Beach, Dr. Cave Beach and Cornwall Beach. Dr Cave's Beach is the best, it is clean and well maintained. There is also a place where yu can buy food on the beach, such as patties, or jerk chicken and the prices are reasonable. There will be a Carnival on Tuesday night and a dance next Friday night at the end of the street".

I started to relax—my caution was unsubstantiated. She proceeded with her discourse:

"Now, Jamdung Tourline provides tours at very special rates. There will be people in the hotel trying to encourage to go on their tours, but I am your representative, you should really call me if you are interested in going on any of the tours - see my number here."

She handed me an unofficial piece of paper with a brief typed description of each tour and the price in pencil. Her telephone number and name clumsily hand-written at the right hand corner of the page.

"... now, 'have you been to Negril Beach? (not waiting for an answer) Ocho Rios? Would yu like to go to Kingston? or there is a beach party on Friday for US$45 where yu can eat and drink as much as yu like?" She waited for a response. I realised it was important for her to add the word "U.S." when referring to dollars to ensure that the prices she was quoting were not misrepresented. She had rekindled my scepticism.

"45 U.S?" It was the first time I had made a sound during her protracted address. [I could go and see Michael Jackson for that amount!]

"Negril is US$40 and Ocho Rios is US$45, she continued, "would you be interested in any of the tours? Oh, and Kingston is US$60.

I was dumbfounded.. the prices were extortionate and conveniently quoted in US dollars to sound reasonable to victims who instinctively had Jamaican dollars in mind. I was marginally interested in the beach party that sounded pretty interesting, maybe I could meet some people there. I told her I would think about it and get back to her.

She seemed slightly agitated: "Yu don't want to go on h'eny of the tours?" transforming her dialect.

"My Auntie is meeting me so I am not sure what plans she has made for me".

"Well enjoy yuh holiday" (a comment that lacked sincerity).

It was useful to know where I could buy the postcards and the stamps. I would get them first thing in the morning, it was too late now.

I had a bath and retired early. I was exhausted.

DISREGARDED AND INTRODUCED

The next day I went to the Seagull Restaurant and ordered some lunch. As I entered, I noticed a coach load of people dismounting courtesy buses that had brought them from their respective hotels. They were being guided to the entrance of the Seagull Restaurant.

"Thank Goodness I arrived in time, I thought, at least I will get served before this lot".

I stood up before the sign that said "please wait to be seated".

A long line had accrued behind me. A tuxedo-clad waiter walked in the general direction of the line, and who I thought was going to direct me to my seat, but instead, he walked passed me and started seating the customers from the back of the line. To add insult to injury, a lesser-clad waiter (short red jacket, no tie) came and directed me to the "bar". I couldn't believe it.

I looked at my reflection, which did not justify what had just happened. I was too stupefied to complain. In 1993, was this really happening – reverse tourism? The rumour that the white tourists tipped better than the black tourists is what denoted priority. As I was black and did not look much like a tourist in my 'daisy-dukes2' and t-shirt, I was doubly jeopardized.

I seated myself at the bar and waited until someone came back to serve me. If their food hadn't acquired such a good reputation, and if I had been more familiar with the district, and if I had a car, and if I had more money, and if the hotel restaurant had not been so expensive, I would have ate somewhere else!

Malicious in intent, I decided not to leave a tip; that would teach them a lesson and satisfy their stupid prediction about blacks not tipping!

It was an angular-faced, young and unassuming waiter that attended to me. So comely and unassertive was he, that he assuaged my anger.

He left me a glass of ice water while I waited for my order to arrive, and I had drunk it ravenously. On observing that my glass empty, and sensing my longing, he brought a large jug full of clear ice water to my table. I appreciated that.

With a sincere smile, my plate of food was strategically placed before me. A flush of forgiveness came over me, and after digesting the sweet tasting food, I awarded him with US$5 tip and left.

After eating my lunch, I oppressed my stomach with the remainder of water in the jug, and decided to allow my food to digest by walking to the beach.

The beach was a few yards away from the post office. Loiterers rallied around outside:

"Yu waan't an escort on the beach, ma'am?"

"No, thank you" I curtly replied.

(The one that asked me looked like he needed an escort himself, but to a shower or a jailhouse!).

There was $22.50 admission fee. A notice read:

"No radios, no drinks, no food, no drugs allowed on the beach. Noisy patrons or those causing a disturbance to others will be ejected immediately"

I paid my money and went inside. There were not many people on the beach, but a few of the local people congregated on the upper level, which was inaccessible without an entrance fee.

I located a level concrete platform and territorially claimed it as my space. I spread my towel out and lay down on it and used my knapsack for a pillow, put on my sunglasses and closed my eyes.

"Mmmm, total peace and quiet—no one to bother me, no phone ringing, no one to answer to, just sheer and ultimate bliss in the sun" I thought. My burnished skin glowed in the sunlight.
The sun beat me mercilessly with an ejaculation of sultry rays. It was not a personal attack - the sun clouted everyone who crossed her path until they became weak, dehydrated and exhausted. Like the masochist I had become, I endured the sweltering heat—sweat cascading from me like rain plummeting through an old roof.

TORMENT 'PON TORMENT

I had been given a book to read as a present. It was entitled: "Women on Top" by Nancy Friday. I took it out of my knapsack and continued reading it.

Erotic undulations radiated out of the book and sent stimulating currents through me. I closed the book.

A voice mercifully intruded on my train of thought. The sensations subsided:

"A weh yu fram?"

My mother's influence took hold and made me judgemental.

I winced at the coarse dialect and unrefined tone. I opened my eyes to see an wide cavernous mouth entrenched in thick overhanging lips. His eyes enigmatically obscured by dark glasses. As he turned to look out into the ocean, I noticed that what should have been the white of his eyes, were a mangy orange. I shuddered. Out of all the people on the beach (I looked around) why come to me? Why not seek someone of his own calibre?

I gave him credit for his brazen boldness. Had the situation been reversed I would have never approached someone as fine as I felt I was. I sat up to evaluate myself. It had to be the braids - they needed redoing, or maybe taking out altogether. I slid my fingers through them and two of them got caught in my fingernail and came away from my head. I shoved them into my bag quickly, hoping that he would not notice the synthetic entrails as this might induce further conversation, which I preferred to avoid.

My braids were starting to look like unkempt dreadlocks and maybe it was their appearance that encouraged this type of person to encroach on my time and space. I examined my nails discriminately. I was in dire need of a manicure. I scrutinized my toes with discern. The varnish was chipped. Assuaging my disdain and accepting partial responsibility for my fate, I decided to entertain his imbecilic exchange.

I analysed his skeletal anatomy—he looked emaciated. His skin had turned white from the sea water, and he looked undernourished yet still strong. His muscles flexed under tight skin.

"Excuse me, missee, a weh yu fram?"

["missee?" so colonial!] Brought up to be courteous, I asked for clarification:

"Do you want to know where I was born, or where my parents come from, or where I live?"
I was hoping that my speaksy spokey accent would throw him off.

"Ah weh yu bawn den?"

The emphasis on the word 'born,' made me wince again before responding.

"I was born in England of Jamaican parents."

"So a H'englan yu live?"

"No, I live in America."

"So why yu don't swim?" he said changing the subject.

"Because I can't swim."

"me can teach yu fe swim"

"Really?" I said sarcastically, "well I'm not interested in learning to swim right now."

"Look pon de sea ma'am.. yu don't see how beautiful it is? Look pon de pickney dem a play in a de water.. yu don' wish yu could swim...? the water coooool and nice. If yu cum h'early tomorro, me wi teach yu fe swim", he said convincingly.

Admittedly I would have loved to learn to swim and should have been grateful for the service. Had my teacher been a tall, clean cut, strong, handsome, virile, well-spoken man, I might have taken advantage of the offer, but this was not the case.

I had to admit, the water did look cool and nice. I pondered for a moment imagining being escorted by a virile man who would swim out into the sea with me on his back. Someone who would pull me towards him and know instinctively how to.... I was lurched into reality. Jamaica had a way of evoking sensuous thoughts.

"Deh is a dance later pon 'roof top' downtown, yu wan' walk wid me go deh?"

I shook my head

"Yu safe yu know... no-one naah kidnap yu — yu deh wid yuh people dem" he implored.

"No, it's alright, thank you", I responded politely.

"Pure ole time music, Sugar Minott, Pat Kelly, Slim Smith.. yu know dem artists deh?" he persisted.

[Of course I knew those artists and I loved their music].

I knew I would enjoy myself had the propositioner been more attractive—I wouldn't be seen dead with this one) - I drifted back into consciousness.

"No, I really cannot go".

I used the opportunity to ask him about the beach party.

"The tour guide at the hotel, informed me about a beach party on Friday night. Do you know anything about the beach parties? How do they regulate people coming on an open beach, and how come they charge US$45?"

"Well iz a private ting for touriss... Dem 'ave a gate and people 'ave fe pay fe get in. Dem play likkle music still, dem mek hole heap o' money aff h'it.."

I was disappointed that it would just be tourists, I thought there would be indigenous Jamaicans on the beach joining in. I decided not to go, besides, hopefully I would be with Uriah, who was someone I knew from School but who had recently decided to live in Jamaica.

"So, yu a come back tomorrow so me can teach yu fe swim?"

"No, I don't think so," I declined politely.

Although he seemed innocuous, I dared not challenge him with harsh words. His intrusion on my privacy continued to frustrate me, although I refused to allow his persistence to drive me from the beach. This situation warranted apprehension and my adherence to the British code of decency would not allow me to express how inconvenienced I felt. Someone called him and he went away.

"Thank Goodness he's gone" I whispered.
I tried to relax again, putting on my dark glasses, recognising just how

prejudice and pompous I was.

"Wa'appen, African Dawta?"

"Oh, no! not again."

"Yu look nice in yuh cut-up cut-up jeans, sista."

I opened my eyes. The voice came from a coolie-dread - his dread-locks tied up with a bright coloured towel. His complexion was a gin-ger-biscuit brown; his form defined.

He wore frayed baggy jeans (probably imported from America) and no shirt.

He grinned, assured of his 'pretty smile':

"So yu a enjoy de beach?"

"Yes, I am enjoying it" I said, disaffected by his pleasantry and no-ticeably good looks [and I would enjoy it better if I was left alone]. "Yu deh pon yu own?"

I wished that I wasn't, but I was, and I admitted it.

"So, is what yu a do later? Yu waan go a 'roof-top?', dem play some nice music"

"Someone else just invited me there"

"Ooo? de bwoy me see a talk to yu, de one dem call Mikey?"

"We didn't exchange names."

"Well, dih one marga bwoy me see a tawk to yu earlier, is him invite yu?"

"Yes" I said, rather embarrassed.

"So, yu a go wid him?"

"No, of course not!"

"So, yu no waan go wid me?" he asked as though he was an obvious alternative.

"No, I don't want to go with anybody"

"Wah? Yu don' come 'ere fe enjoy yuself?"

"Yes, but I can enjoy myself on my own, thank you!"

"Pon yu own? So yu sinting naa scratch yu?"

Sensing my disgust, he continued:

"Well if yu change yu mine, me a go dyah"

[Yes, roaming the beach, you no-good layabout!].

He walked away defeated. He knew I would not be back.

Time passed and 'marga Mikey' returned with a large green leaf, spewing out gooey substance.. which, unauthorized, he rubbed on my shoulders:

"Ah dih real ting dis. Aloe—good fih yu skin, proteck yu from dih sun".

For a moment I forgot who he was and what he looked like. The substance felt cool and refreshing on my shoulders. It was very considerate of him to go out of his way to make sure my skin was protected. I took advantage of his temporal kindness, forgetting the contemptible thoughts of a few moments past.

When the leaf was dry, he got up and beseeched:

"Ay tooriss - a twenty dollars fe dis yu know. Let me know if yu waan' some—me 'haffee see if me can mek some money off it".

[Well, you definitely are not getting any money from me for that little dirty piece of green leaf—probably picked it up off the beach anyway, and come to think of it, my shoulders didn't even feel cool, and they felt uncomfortably sticky! And fancy calling me a tourist, how did he know I wasn't born in Jamaica? This was service I could do without].

He got the hint that I was not paying for it and walked off. I decided I would go and get something to drink.

I passed a little hut that advertised mango juice, fruit punch and other things. "Mmmmm, fruit punch". I asked them how much it was and they told me JD45 dollars.

I had stopped thinking in Jamaican dollars, it was the American dollar I used as my yardstick to determine whether or not the price was fair. I surmised that drinking and eating in Jamaica was quite expensive but JD$45 dollars for a glass of healthy fruit punch was very reasonable.

I was allowed to chaperone the fusion of fruit into juice and watched her put in pieces of banana, papaya, sour sop, watermelon and some other relatively insignificant bits of fruit (no mango) and then liquidize them together in an electric blender.

To test the consistency and taste, the lady dipped a spoon in the concoction and tipped some into the palm of her hand so she could taste it. I liked the way she did that. My mother always did that when she tasted the soup she was making [I didn't see people do that much anymore in England]. Seeing this woman demonstrate a similar technique to that of my mother, reassured me that it would taste just right.

Satisfied with her composition, she poured it out into a long glass and handed it to me and waited for my approval. I exchanged the JD$45 after confirming its validity with a large smile. It was as thirst quenching and as tastily nutritious as I had expected it to be. I guzzled it down hungrily, and then proceeded to the Seagull where I would have dinner.

EARTH AND CULTURE

On the way to the Seagull, a jungle of woodcarvings scattered on the ground mesmerized me. There was no symmetry, no order, and no proportion, just carvings placed at random on the earth.

I was attracted to one piece in particular, and being an artist, myself, I appreciated the skill that had gone into a carving shaped like a tree. On the boughs, birds carved to precision, sanded down to a smooth finish and polished to a glimmering honey-coloured sheen and placed on the branches. I marvelled at the intricacy.

"Yu wan' dat?" A voice emanated from nowhere disturbing my equilibrium. I glared at her. [How dare she encroach upon this sacred moment!] I tried to play the native's role:

"How much fe it?"

"A 20 U.S. dollars dat"

So much for me trying to talk like a native, it didn't work. [20 US dollars indeed — that was equivalent to 500 Jamaican dollars!]. I was beginning to notice that conversion of prices varied depending on which price sounded more inviting. If the US currency made it seem cheaper they would quote in US currency, and if, by quoting Jamaican currency, it made it seem like a bargain, the same tactic applied.
She was making my decision to purchase very difficult. I was battling with her aggressive tone, innate culture, and my admiration for the carving."I'm thinking about it", I remarked, reinstating my refined accent.

The oscillation of accents was becoming tiresome and definitely not working to my advantage. I replaced the carving and walked off.

'Wa'appen? Yu don' want it?"

I looked at her exasperatingly. I did want it. I was expecting her to call me back and negotiate a lower price, but I had walked about 50 yards, slowly and deliberately towards the exit, giving her a chance to reduce her price, but she had not called me back. I stopped myself at the corner. 20 US? I questioned myself. It was definitely worth it, but I knew I could get it cheaper 'downtown'. Would I get the opportunity to go 'downtown', though? That was another question.

I wrestled with indecision for a while. I decided to buy it. I went back and picked it up, looking at it one last time. It was definitely a good piece of artwork. I gave her the money. "Yu don' want any t-shirt? — 12 U.S. fe dem"[Now, that was definitely a rip off! 12 U.S? The prices of t-shirts, I knew about.]

"Come look pon dem na" she insisted.

"No thank you" I replied and left.

I was happy with my purchase until I heard that I could have bought it for US$5 in Freeport, and I became resentful [Why did I tend to lose out on bargains – it was so annoying?]

The resentment didn't last, my appreciation returned and I nursed my purchase before packing it away in the suitcase.

TELEPHONE SERVICE

It was about 5.30 in the evening, I returned to the Seagull Restaurant, more out of convenience than anything else.

I looked at the menu - everything was over JD$100 dollars. I noticed a vegetarian meal for JD$95 — I would try that. It was sautéed callaloo, mashed potato and rice and peas. It didn't sound very appetizing but when I ate it, it was delicious. Because the food was so good, I ate at the Seagull in the morning, for breakfast, in the afternoon, for lunch, and in the evening, for dinner.

I learned that they had 'specials' which were cheap meals, standard breakfasts, etc. so I always ended up having the 'specials'. I was such a frequent patron that the waiters didn't even have to ask me what I wanted, they just used to explain what the 'special' was, and it would always be to my liking both economically and in taste.

I went back to my room in the hotel and looked through the rules and regulations that were on the dresser set out in a report-like format: 'No visitors allowed in the guest rooms; turn off lights and air conditioners to save electricity, how to get room service, how to make a phone call', etc. I threw myself backwards onto the bed. This is the life I thought. What a delight to be alone... to get away from creeps like those I met on the beach.

The appreciation of isolation didn't last very long. I soon became bored and restless. Who should I call? Uriah? Auntie Sonia? my nephew Winston? cousin David? I had so many choices. I mused a while. Who should I see first? David. I had not heard from him for thirteen years... I would call him.

I dialled zero for the operator:

"Yes?"

"Could you get me.."

"..'hole' on a minute"

I was interrupted in mid-sentence, and after a few minutes:

"Yes?" the voice came back, "What was dat number yu h'arsk me fa?"

"I would like you to get..."

"Sorry, hole on a minute"

I had been waiting for at least five minutes, by which time my anger had mounted. I heeded their laughing in the background and slammed the phone down.

I remembered seeing a questionnaire requesting a rating of the services provided by the hotel. I immediately retrieved it and the section under phone service, I wrote 'unsatisfactory'.

My phone rang:

"Wah number yu said yu did want?"

I couldn't stand it. Had they received no training on how to speak properly? Where was the telephone etiquette? the courtesy? The motto that the customer comes first? Basic professionalism? Were these ingredients not important anymore? If I had another method of contacting Kingston I would have done so, but it was not so easy to obtain phone cards, which would have been my only alternative at that particular time.

After gaining composure I repeated the number:

"Yu know dis is a long-distance number?"

I felt like saying 'what the hell has it got to do with you?

I must know it is a long distance number because I gave it to you –
Duhhhhh! It is your job to get me the number, not ask questions?
Voices raced around in my head, but I kept silent.

"Is a long-distance number yu know, yu still want it?" she repeated
expecting me to confirm that it was ok for her to call the number.
[Typical, when precision was of no consequence that was the time it
was applied].

'Yes. I do!" I answered shortly.

I was constantly in dissension with who I was and who I had become.

The line rang. Someone picked up:

"Could I speak to David please, I'm his Auntie"

"Sorry, David doesn't live here any more"

"Do yu know where he lives?"

"No!"

The force with which she replaced the receiver disturbed me.

Oh well, at least there was Uriah. He had said he would be only too
willing to come and pick me up and take me around as soon as I arrived. All I had to do was call him.

I relaxed with that confirmation.

CHOICE NOT CIRCUMSTANCE

Uriah was a Rasta. He used to live in England and immigrated to Jamaica shortly after leaving school. We had kept in touch over the years through letters and more recently, through email. Uriah was very good looking and it seemed that every time he visited England he ended up getting some woman pregnant. When the 'baby muddas' pressured him for money or emotional support, he would return to Jamaica calling me beforehand to say "Myrns, me cyaan stan dih pressure, me gaan."

Apart from the four daughters he had in London, he had two sons for a woman in Jamaica and one for an American tourist. Despite his shenanigans, Uriah was a good friend to me and we talked a lot. I would call Uriah in the morning.

I had a bath and went to bed. I tried to sleep, but I couldn't. I wasn't going to call Auntie Sonia until the following week, but I was restless. I called her number:

"Sorry, she 'as gone to dih country fih a week to a funeral—did she know yu was comin?" the voice rang dimly in my ears.

"No, she didn't. I was going to surprise her." I mumbled nonplussed.

I replaced the receiver without leaving a number where I could be contacted. What was the point, if she wasn't coming back until next week, when I would be leaving? I needed her now.

This holiday was not turning out how I expected. I mean, I did say I wanted to spend the first week alone, but that was meant to be out of choice, not out of circumstance.

"Next week?" I couldn't believe it. I slumped back on the bed, started reading the book again which ceased to comfort me.

I got up and stepped out onto the patio. It had turned dark. The sea's hue had changed from china blue to a hazy black. Silver-grey highlights made the sea even more beautiful in the evening mist, like a fluorescent blanket shimmering towards the horizon. I felt a slight irritation and slapped my shoulder: " bloody mosquitoes".

I went back inside and turned on the television.

Good, a movie on HBO. I started watching a movie until I dozed off, leaving the television on. "Damn" I whispered to my guilt-ridden sub-conscious, "I should turn the television off to save electricity." I did not want to get up. I knew that if I did, I would never be able to re-capture this relaxed state of mind again. I drifted off. ".. the tel-e-vi-sion... the tel-e-vi-son..". my conscience hauntingly echoed.

A RIDE TO BROWNS TOWN

In the morning, I called Uriah. "So wha yu a do?" he asked me.

I thought it was strange that he should ask me that when he had asked me to call him on my arrival.

"Nothing" I said.

"So when yu arrive?"

"I arrived yesterday".

I was feeling uncomfortable because I had informed him of my dates before I left and he had obviously forgotten.

"So wah? Yu wan' come up ya?" (he asked, passing the responsibility of choice to me).

"That was what we had planned, wasn't it?" I asked somewhat concerned at his non-retentive memory.

"Well, me car naa work yu know, me 'ave fe tek it to Kingston fih get fix. Is how deh-deh fah?"

Feeling desperate and troubled and knowing that if he didn't take me out I would have a lonely weekend, I decided to speed up the programme. I only had one more option left, and that was Winston who I had wanted to save until the very last, for my own reasons.

"Well I am supposed to meet Auntie Sonia on Friday, so I only have today and tomorrow to see you and Miss Ouida". Uriah rented a room in Miss Ouida's home. Miss Ouida used to live in England, and my mother had taken me to see her one time over Christmas so I knew her a little bit.

"Well me will see what me can do. Mih wih call you tomorrow".

"Thanks a million", I mumbled under my breath with sarcasm.

Early, the next morning, Uriah called confirming that he would be at my hotel by 9.30 that morning. I was relieved and surprised and calculated that he would arrive around 10.30. He actually arrived at 11.25. No apologies for lateness and I did not take umbrage because his behaviour conflicted with my code of ethics – I was relieved to see him.

When I saw the car coast into the driveway, I noticed a protruding muscular arm and smiled with approval. I didn't realize it was Uriah until he got out. I ran downstairs, happy to meet a familiar face at last. He was not as affectionate as he was in London - he stiffened when I reached to hug him. I pretended not to notice and went outside. There was a man in the car who smiled at me—he introduced him as 'his bredren'.

On the way to Brownstown he kept saying he was hungry. I wasn't sure whether he was hinting that I should buy some food for him or what.

"Yuh don' hungry?"

"Well, not really, I said disguising the truth. I can wait until I reach Brownstown. Miss Ouida would probably put on something special for me to eat".

He pulled over sharply into a ditch so that the car was as far off the road as possible and got out. There was a hut across the road where mangoes of different sizes were spread out. (I loved mangoes!). I squeezed myself out of the door, which was wedged against a rock, (since to get out of the driver's side would be to commit suicide) and went over to the hut. The Rasta who owned the 'store' had one of those faces that you recognize, but can't remember where from.

I picked up one of the mangoes, it had JD$20 label neatly stuck on it. (At least I didn't get the feeling I was being exploited.) I took up three and was just about to give him the $60 when Uriah stopped me:

"No, man, we mus can get dem cheaper up soh.."

"Are you sure?" I asked.

"Yeh, mon.. but if yu really feel fe a mango, jus buy one".

I bought one. It was a nice big one and it smelt ripe. I couldn't wait to buy some more.

He drove recklessly for what seemed like hours, deciding not to over-take until he approached a bend, exaggerating his swerves to avoid potholes and dead goats. I wish I had sat in the back of the car crouched in sleep so I did not have to see the miraculous swerving from gullies that pleaded for corpses. Just one swerve too far to the left or to the right and we would have been delivered prematurely to our graves.

He stopped again:

"Yuh wan' some sugar cane?"

I saw him reaching into his back pocket for money, so I nodded. Then he asked his bredren if he had any change.

He got out of the car with his bredren and came back with two sugar canes, one for me and one for himself. We chewed them for the du-ration of the journey. It made a change being treated, even if it was just to a piece of sugar cane. I was appreciative.

"Dem seh Jamaica small—yu tink it small?" Uriah asked.

After driving for two hours, it definitely did not seem small to me, I said to myself rather than to him.

"Brownstown is over 90 miles from Montego Bay"

"But I thought you said it wasn't far, when I called you. You said you would come to pick me up as if it was around the corner?" I quizzed.

"It no far really... Kingston is 150 miles away from Montego Bay."

I was really beginning to appreciate the way Uriah had gone out of his way to come and pick me up. No wonder he didn't arrive at the hotel until 11.25! I didn't realize he was coming from such a distance. I would never have arranged for him to come and pick me up had I known. Anyway, he was here and he didn't seem to mind as he travelled with fury to reach his destination. Uriah was a Scorpio, he challenged danger.. a risk taker... the drive confirmed this.

Just before we reached Brownstown, Uriah hailed two old ladies as if he knew them. They were standing by a bush, under the shade of a tree. They were selling mangoes which had been separated on a cardboard box according to size, and priced accordingly. On enquiring, we found out that the prices ranged from $10 for the very small ones to $35 for the large ones (the same size I had paid $20 for earlier on!). .

"Dem too teef man" Uriah exclaimed "..we can get better and cheaper mangos up soh".

"Up soh, weh? H'eny weh yu go, a de same price" the lady retorted.

"I don' tink we can get dem h'eny cheaper, yu know, dread" his bredren said (speaking for the first time).

i wish I hadn't listened to him. If I had followed my mind, I would have had some nice julie mangoes to eat later. As it happened, is one soh-soh mango I bought.

That is the problem, when you visit as a 'tourist', you rely on indigenous people to guide you. You assume they know what they are talking about; that they know 'the runnings', when really, one's instinct is more reliable.

That happened to me quite a lot in Jamaica, where I depended on the expertise of the locals, and rather than admit they didn't know, they would lead me up the garden path. It was so annoying.

The thing is, they were so convincing - you would never know, they didn't know what they were talking about - they spoke so assertively, It was as if they really knew the place they were describing - or where something was - when they didn't know squat!

I definitely thought my cousin, new the area, and when he said, "more up soh" - he was sure there were more 'up soh', I could get.

I think he was embarrassed he had let me down. Humiliation drove the car to Browns Town.

ME BELLIE A BAWL!

Somewhat shaken up, I eventually arrived at Miss Ouida's house in Brownstown.

She was happy to see me. Her face was beaming.

However, I was not impressed with Uriah's 'apartment' (which is where I would sleep if I had to stay the night).

He was a D.J. so his room was full of records and equipment. His surroundings illustrated that he was a man without a female to indulge him. No clean bathroom towels; the toilet bowl had not been flushed; his pillowcases were dingy grey and the bedspreads looked shabby.

I went on a mental expedition. Why did I leave Montego Bay and the comfort of my hotel room, fe dis? There were times that only patois could express the way I felt.

"Yu should-a never check into a hotel.." Uriah said, contradicting my thoughts while simultaneously shaking his head with disapproval.

Miss Ouida reaffirmed proudly:

"Yes, it would be better fe yu fe stay here, h'even if it mean seh de two a we fe sleep pon dih floor".
"I don't think so!" I thought vehemently. I looked down at floor, uneven tiles jutted out belligerently through the threadbare covering.

" We would be only too glad to 'ave yu stay here.."

[I bet you would!] my silent voice challenged.

I knew that if I had stayed with them instead of booking into a hotel, my conscience would have made me contribute US$100 dollars to help towards the food and other incidentals. While staying in a hotel, I had no obligation and that was how I liked it.

The invitation seemed charitable, but as far as I was concerned, the underlying motives were questionable.

"Me bellie a bawl, me a go dead fe hungry. Me no h'eat from morning, yu know!" Uriah moaned.

Miss Ouida kissed her teeth.

When most Jamaicans wanted to emphasise an emotion, they would add an 'h' in front of a vowel.

"H'eny food deh roun' yah, Miss Ouida?"

Miss Ouida kissed her teeth again and turned her back.

"Yu put h'eny food inside yah?" she responded.
"Cha, Miss Ouida, no gwaan soh!"

After an almost three hour journey, he was hungry and my stomach started rumbling too.

Miss Ouida could have filled up the cupboards with food because she was receiving a healthy pension, but she knew that Uriah would take advantage and would come and 'nyam her out', so she preferred to keep her personal supply in her room. As far as she was concerned, if he wanted food he could go to 'one of his women dem' or work and buy it put in the house. I can't say I blamed her for thinking like that.

Poverty was relative and superficial. She had to pretend that 'she couldn't manage' so he wouldn't exploit her situation, but it didn't make a difference – he didn't even business whether there was food there or not, as long as he could get his hands on some "flour, sugar and water fe mek two dumplin", but I was about to be penalised for his lack of contribution.

Uriah was in the kitchen opening all the cupboards and kissing his teeth at their bareness. He opened the fridge and took out a 'chuka-chuka' plastic bag that contained two so-so slices of bread. He put it back and looked once more inside the cupboards to see if he had missed anything at the back of the cupboard. He was standing on tiptoe this time. I saw him reach inside to the back of one of the cup-boards. He had located a tin of something.
"Myrns, yuh 'ave any petrol money? Me don' 'ave any gas in me car, yuh know"

I would have preferred if had told me beforehand that he would love to collect me but he would need petrol. My nature would have given him petrol anyway, but I didn't like the idea of him transferring the lift to my auntie to an excuse to ask me for money.

I should have realised really – it was a very long ride and for a quasi-local to do that charitably would have been asking a bit too much. He was obviously providing a service and expected to get paid.

"How much is gas?" I gave him JA100 dollars without waiting for a response, but his expression signified it was insufficient. I gave him another 100-dollar bill, his sullenness lifted. "Give Tanks.. Jah Rasta-fari, Selassi I" I gave him a further US$20:

"It's not much, but it might help". I said.

"Give Praises to Jah Rastafari, Conquering Lion on the Tribe of Judah, Elect of God..." he chanted with respect and appreciation while ab-sent-mindedly groping his protuberance. The US$ bill made him feel happier.

He opened the tin of sardines and mixed it with haphazardly chopped onions. He then took out the dry bread from the fridge and a bottle of hot pepper.
"A Miss Ouida favourite bread dis" he said cheerfully, waving the two slices that were left.

"Yu wan' some a dis?" (pointing to the dish that contained the sardines in tomato sauce).

I wasn't sure whether I should— Miss Ouida's favourite bread and the last two pieces? But then, what was the alternative?

My stomach had grown accustomed to the Seagull's regular breakfasts, lunches and dinners, it was reverberating inside. The sardines were served on a timeworn chipped dish—a gooey red substance with grey mounds, and fish bones resembling strands of hair, jutted out precariously. I ate it nonetheless, and the saying that 'anything tastes good when your hungry' was false.

Miss Ouida arrived from somewhere and threw some desiccated looking yams on the large wooden table.

"Dem bwoy will 'ave fe cook de food yu know, becaw me naa cook... me foot tired... If me never 'ave fe send dem bwoy go a school h'an if Uriah was working, I could live like a queen, but I don't get a penny from h'eny o dem." she lamented bitterly.

I was surprised at her martyrdom.

"Why don't you kick them out?" I said, scathingly
"Uriah look h'after me – me need a man inna de house, yu know, and besides, me feel sorry fe dem" she defended.

Uriah's cousins were living in the house too - biological cousins and adopted ones – in all there were four grown men ranging from 17 to

25 years old living in the house.

"What happens when they start to have girlfriends?" I quizzed.

"Girlfrien'? Girlfrien'? [she repeated for emphasis] Girlfrien'? hah-hey! dem 'ave girlfrien' already. A young men dem, (she proudly admitted) dih gal dem come fram all over dih place fe see dem.. dih phone don' stop ring... A sweet bwoy dem me 'ave here, yu know." she said with a smile that revealed a gold crown between her two front teeth. I listened inattentively. So why complain I thought.

URIAH—KING ROYAL

I excused myself from her presence and went into the back room where Uriah was preparing the large sound system. He was arching backward, fingers nuzzling in his knotted beard while his hand supported his elbow in a contemplative stance.

"What's wrong?" I asked concerned.

"Me don't know wha fih do fe get it fih work.."

"But I thought it was your sound system?"

"It is, but dis ting 'ave too much button pon it!"

He straightened up and touched something. A loud buzzing noise belched from within the large frame.

"Aaaah, h'it a come!"

He lifted the arm off of the turntable and set it on the record but there was no sound. He resumed his former stance, and then suddenly he pulled off his hat, as if to free his dreadlocks would provide the answer.

"Gi I-an-I wisdom, Oh Jah!"

He pressed another button... the equipment groused and then, as if pandering to its owner's touch, it purred silently.

"Selassi-I"

Uriah smiled, raising his hands above his head as if to acknowledge His Royal Majesty; [It made a change seeing someone with nice teeth, whether or not they were false didn't matter, they looked good]. A loud boom suspended my admiration. The music had started.

Uriah felt secure enough, now, to leave the record playing unsupervised. A lavish billow of smoke clouded the room violating my nostrils in the process giving off a distinct scent. The wave of smoke danced around the room and Uriah with it, gyrating his hips and synchronizing his movements with the melody. He tossed his head from side to side, quaking his long locks until they wrapped around his face. The image captured was like that of a print you might see of Bob Marley in an art gallery. The record simmered to a halt, and he put on another one, turning up the volume simultaneously.

Disconcerted I asked him if Miss Ouida didn't mind the loud music and the repugnant smell of tobacco in her house:

"No mon, me Miss Ouida cool, yu know—a my likkle apartment dis—a two room me 'ave".

I examined his 'apartment' - a garage which had been converted by erecting a wall, cutting out a window and putting down a piece of carpet, transforming this contrivance into his empire. Distinguished prints of Bob Marley and a brass framed photograph of Haile Selassi gave his empire perspective.

Rotating his head to the rhythm, I watched his tapered frame buck symmetrically. The haze was now very dense causing it to affect my discernment. I too, swayed to the music:

"A me soun' system dis. Mih call it 'King Royal' H'it big out here", he said confidently adjusting the base line.

"H'Uriah!!" Miss Ouida hollered [It was always H'Uriah and not Uriah when she was angry], jolting me back to sobriety, "Ton dung de music!!" Uriah was preoccupied, he didn't hear her. I shook him and he looked at me with reddened eyes through his wire-rimmed pre-scriptioned spectacles, and smiled.

"Miss Ouida is getting upset. She said you should turn down the music"

"Miss Ouida h'easy mon, she h'easy like h'a Sunday marnin'. H'eny-way, h'after de music no loud" he whispered in a tone of abstemious-ness.

He placed a protective arm around his sound-system.
"Don't worry, mon, she coool—coool like dis spliff yah!" he continued in response to my fretful expression.

"Me, seh, h'Uriah, tun dun de music, or tun h'it arf!!" she yelled.

She definitely didn't sound 'coool' to me.

I left his domain, and went back into the kitchen [I didn't want her to think I was conspiring with him].

"Me can't tan de bangarang! H'it ah gimmee blood pressure!" she groaned.

[Uriah obviously didn't realize that she was affected by the loud music].

"Dat boy a gimmee headache. H'all him know fe do is fe stink up me house wid him tobacco, h'an mek noise... He would not h'even lift a finger fe help me inna de house h'an him know dat me leg dem a gimmee trouble Me need 'im fe 'elp me!"

I minute ago she was telling me she couldn't do without him, when I told her to kick him out. I thought he was paying rent. He obviously wasn't.

I felt like saying to her, why don't you ask him to help you then. Men, by their innate nature adopt a behavioural strategy to get out of doing things – some call it 'learned incompetence'. I was sure that had he realized the smoke, the loud music, and the burdensome presence of his acquired siblings was adversely affecting Miss Ouida's health, he would have done something about it. Uriah was not calculating. He had known Miss Ouida for years and I am sure he cared about her. He was, admittedly, taking advantage of a situation because Miss Ouida was allowing him to do so. He was making the most of his unlicensed freedom, but his behaviour wasn't wilful.

A CONFLICT WITH STATUS

Miss Ouida suffered from fluid retention. Her swollen hand cupped her forehead. Her hairline was receding and her curly perm needed retouching as did her grey hairs.

The dress [that looked too tight for her] looked aged, and her loosely hung legs looked more distended than usual.

She didn't look like the Miss Ouida I had met in England, but seemed consoled by my presence. A young woman was out the back washing clothes. Miss Ouida had acquired a maid. Having a helper gave one status. When she remembered the maid, she immediately became excited. She was no longer slovenly but a renewed energy became her. The stiff and tired legs became animated in her eagerness to introduce the maid to me. As she led me to the garden she spoke in an effervescent manner. I couldn't believe the transformation. She obviously wanted me to carry the news back to my mother that she had her own maid.

"Yu want to see all de clothes she wash since morning. I employ her from 6 in the morning until 4.00 in the afternoon. I don't really 'ave to watch her yu know, she is very good.

She guided me to the front yard and to the line of clothes that were hanging out there, admiring them as though she had washed them herself:

"I give her JD$75 a day fe dis".

[$75 a day... that is just under US$4, I calculated].

"Jus look how many jeans she wash, she wuk hard yuh see, bless her soul. I don' know how I woulda manage wid out her. Seventeen pairs of jeans yu know. She start from h'early morning. Dem boys just pile up de clothes dem h'an gi 'er fe wash... she good yu know... she just wash h'everyting and bring my special clothes dem in separate.

"So this wasn't all. I counted the pieces on the line. 17 pairs of jeans, three pairs of slacks, 12 shirts, 17 vests, 14 briefs and that didn't include Miss Ouida's 'special' clothes. Suddenly it seemed appropriate to use the US equivalent to evaluate fairness. Four measly dollars for 8 hours work definitely unfair, and I am sure the poor woman never got a lunch break!

"Yes, me dear, me 'ave me helper" she continued. The loud music didn't seem to disturb her any more.. maybe it wasn't the music that bothered her at all—maybe it was the loneliness. We went back inside.

I learned that Uriah had never assumed responsibilities for his children or their mothers. "Children will be having children" he prophesied. It was time to escape to ultimate freedom (Aunt Ouida). It is a Rasta's right to be free: "Me love Jamaica, is yah so me a-go stay". Miss Ouida took her resentment out on everyone who visited her. She now regretted accommodating selfish grown men who could not devise a means (nor had any intention of devising any) to contribute towards their education and household expenses.

BIG HOUSE H'AN A DEAD FE HUNGRY

Miss Ouida took her indignation out on me. She had no intention of cooking.

"Dem bwoy tek too much liberty. Me no care if dem dead fe hungry, me naa cook fe dem. Dem too wuckless"

[What about me Miss Ouida, what about me!] I challenged silently as my stomach gargled. For some reason Bob Marley's record came to mind... "a hungry man is an angry man..." I was becoming listless and agitated.

My mango! I remembered my mango which subdued my mood. I sliced off the skin with a sharp knife, washed it off, sliced it into little pieces and ate it. It was sweet, juicy and nice. I wish I had bought some more!

On noticing that the 'boys' had not volunteered to cook the neglected yams, she relented and said wearily:

"Would yuh like some ackee 'an saltfish?"

(Would I like some ackee and saltfish? — what a stupid question! Of course I would like some ackee and saltfish, I'm bloody starving!)

Refusing to allow my outward comportment to reflect my inward sentiment, I responded in humble demeanour:
"Yes please, I would love some thank you".
Well me a go see if h'eny of dem bwoy will bwoil some fih yu, udderwise me wi haf fe bwoil it meself!", she mumbled as she shifted reluctantly towards the stove. [It didn't occur to me before how intuitively I understood the lingo.]

Boil some? I thought. How long was this food going to take when she hadn't even started cooking it yet? My stomach continued to snarl in annoyance.

If I knew my niece was coming to visit, I would have been up before dawn making sure she had something to eat on arrival.

"Me don't want yu tellin yuh mudda seh me never feed her one gyal pickney.." She interjected my thoughts. Miss Ouida was right that she didn't want my mother to know. My mother would have never treated Miss Ouida or any member of her family in such a blasé manner, or anyone for that matter! My mother would always rustle up something to give to any visitor, even if it was bully beef and rice (what Jamaicans call "poor-mans food").

I decided that I wanted to go back to Montego Bay. I couldn't stand the 'ole nayga' lifestyle anymore.

I told Uriah that my Auntie was meeting me and that I had to be back to the hotel by 8.00 the following morning. He seemed disappointed: "Go tell Miss Ouida." he said.
I called out to Miss Ouida. I could hear her indiscernible voice through the noise, and followed it.

"Come in, come in.. a fe me room dis…", she said with pride". When I don't want h'eny one fih bodder me, me come inside 'ere". It didn't occur to me before how intuitively I understood the lingo.

She was sitting on her bed, a room draped white nets and ribbons far enhanced than the rest of the house. She was smoking a cigarette.

"I didn't know you smoked". I said, asking rather than stating.

"Yes, I don't smoke much. Me 'ave fe hide dem weh from dih bwoy dem. One pack o' cigarette fif last me one whole week, an yet every day dem bwoy come ask me fih a cigarette h'an me haffee gih dem. If me don't have it, dem wi ask me fe money fih go buy cigarette. I don't know why dem don't mek fih dem cigarette last dem. Anyway is nice fe see yu again. How is yuh mudda?   [I observed that she asked more as an afterthought than out of genuine interest].

"My mother is fine, Miss Ouida. I am so sorry I can't stay over, but I have to go back to the hotel now," I volunteered disingenuously.

"O.K..." she said, almost too eagerly, "...well, me glad me get fe see yu. I would 'ave been so upset fih know seh yu come ah Jamaica h'an me don't get fih see yu. Dat is why me get dis big 'ouse out here, so me people dem can 'ave somewhere fe stay... [and dead fe hungry? I thought]. Well jus mek sure yu get home safe, at lease yu see weh me live. Tell yuh mudda seh me long fe see 'er"

Miss Ouida was determined to show off her 'big house' before I left - the other two bedrooms, the orange tree, although she mentioned: "dey out of season right now".

She guided me toward the front of the house and showed me the unfinished concrete facing that constituted a hazard to the blind:

"Uriah fih finish dat. 'im start it some time ago and don' finish it.."

As if conceding to his habitual lack of conviction, she hollered:

"Uriah, Uriah, come tun off dih water"

[Turn off the water?]

"Why are you turning off the water?" I asked.

"Me 'ave water in dih tank me caan use" [The tank?]

I observed a rusty looking pipe that led into the tank. This was where the water overflowed after accumulating in the gutter from the rain.

Uriah came out and put his hand down a hole in the pathway. I saw him contort himself as he reached down. He jerked a little and withdrew his hand. Then, as if he disowning his hand, he extended it, shaking his fingers free of debris and headed for the bathroom.

BACK TO MONTEGO BAY

He came out shortly afterwards, drying his reclaimed hands with a clean towel he had taken off the line.

"So is wah Miss Ouida seh?"

"She said O.K. What did you expect her to say?"

"Me tawt she would try fe mek yuh stay"

"So iz 8:30 a night now - me naah get back til midnight an me 'ave fe go a Kingston tomarro - h'an me naa drive back by meself.."

[That's right, Uriah, put me on a guilt trip!]

Two girls had converged into Uriah's 'apartment' and had taken over playing the records. They were no more than 16 or 17 years of age. I think they had come to visit Uriah's 'nephews', but 45-year-old Uriah was being overly attentive to them.

When I went in the room to collect my bag [which I had hidden under the bed], they were all sharing what looked like a cigarette.

"Yu wan' come fe a drive?" he asked them.

"Where to?" one asked.
"Montego Bay".

"Dat too far" she responded unconvincingly.

"It not too far, we'll be back by 10.30" (I knew that was not true but I did not interfere with his negotiating plans).

One of the girls looked at her watch and then she looked at her friend. The other nodded. Uriah made eye contact with one of his 'favourite' nephews.. sign language was going on... they were all in-sync. An agreement was reached. Good, I thought, we were in business.

I gave Uriah another JA$200 to take me to the hotel which he prudently placed in his back pocket. Remembering the earlier journey, I got into the back of the car.

It wasn't long before I heard a loud scream. The car swerved in a distorted fashion:

"Me cyaa see man, dem a bline me wid dem headlight!"

"Yu want me fe drive?" asked one of the girls.

"No, man, iz alright, me don' know how dem expect people fe see when dem a bline dem with dem bright light..." he continued nervously.

Now, I not only had gullies, potholes and overtaking at corners to contend with, but under-aged girls (obviously without driving licences) volunteering to drive. Plus Uriah was claiming that he couldn't see! I crouched lower in my seat and whispered the Lord's Prayer.

I must have dozed off because the next thing I knew, we had jolted to a halt. I was told to get out the car, we were getting a drink.

"This a nice nightclub" one of the girls said.

I didn't want to go to a nightclub, I thought, I wanted to get back to the hotel, but I was at their mercy. I hope they were not expecting me to spend any money. Usually, when 'foreigners' are guilt-tripped into spending money. I went inside and gritted my teeth and sat at the bar. There was no one there but the bartender and us. It was pitch black outside.

"So what yu want fih drink?" Uriah asked gallantly waving one of the 100-dollar bills in his hand that I had given him (he was obviously trying to impress the young girls). As he was paying for the drinks, I asked for a soda. "Drinks all roun an' a pack a cigarette" he boasted.

('Drinks all round' my foot. There was only four of us!).

If he was so hard up, why was he spending the money (he had asked me to give him for petrol) on drinks and cigarettes?
"Dih customers dem pay me JA$1400 fe tek dem to Montego Bay" he had mentioned casually earlier, appealing to my conscience. That was why I had given him another JA$200. I figured, what with the US$20 I had also given him, he didn't do too badly, considering I was supposed to be his friend!

After a couple of drinks we all assembled in the car. I crouched again in the back seat. Miraculously, I fell asleep. It was about 10.30 p.m., in the evening when I reached back to the hotel. I went straight to bed, appreciating the hotel more than ever now.

BEACH PARTY

I decided that I would go to the beach party. After spending the equivalent of nearly JA$1000 for the trip to Brownstown, which could have provided me with food for five days, I decided that US$45 was nothing, especially if I enjoyed myself.

I called Genevieve and asked her if there was still time to make a reservation (since it was that same evening); she said she would come over right away for the money.

She arrived within 10 minutes. I asked her if it would look strange me going there by myself, but she assured me that she would be there. I felt better. I parted with my money and she gave me a slip of paper. I thanked her and she told me that the coach would be ready by 6.30 p.m. I got excited. I put on my sexy salmon mini dress, my 'fish-net' sandals and wore my provocative wig.

The bus arrived on time. I boarded, and on looking around, everyone was in t-shirts, shorts and jeans. Dammit, I was over-dressed but it was too late to change.

"Do yu 'ave your receipt?" the driver asked.

"Oh, do I need it?"

"Of course yu need it!"
Accepting that "gruffness" was a part of the culture I conceded.

"Please wait, I have to run upstairs to get it."

I ran upstairs, and pulled everything out to look for this piece of paper I had discarded. It took me a full five minutes to find it. Victorious, I ran downstairs just to see the bus driving off. [What was this? I pay my big-big US$45 and he is ready to drive off and leave me?]

"Yoh!" I shouted, unbefitting of a woman dressed the way I was.

The bus screeched to a halt.

'Couldn't you wait? You knew I was coming?" I snapped.
[But there again, maybe he didn't know I was coming. Maybe he thought I was trying to con a free ride, or that I hadn't really bought a ticket. It was possible].

The evening was already showing signs of mediocrity. Disparagingly, I walked to the back of the bus noticing loving couples all the way to the rear. I did not see Genevieve, either, I was the lone-ranger, sticking out like a parrot among the peacocks.

To make matters worse, my command to ensure that the driver heard me, had labelled me as a 'street gal'. Nobody reciprocated the series of smiles I administered on the way to my seat, in fact, they looked disturbed at the prospect of my participation.

"Mek sure yu get yuh bamboo cup because without yuh bamboo cup yu won't drink as much as yu like", the driver cackled.

The bus driver dropped us off about 5 minutes away (he could have waited) to a dingy beach (especially in the light). There was an old shed where a lady took our receipts and gave us the notorious 'bamboo jug' the driver had told us about, in return. [One half-dead bamboo cup for US$45!] The platform for the entertainers was being prepared. The food was just arriving.

"One word of advice... drink some of the hot pepper pot soup, so yu don't get drunk", shouted the driver, as if trying to create a mood of festivity.

The tourists dismounted the bus and looked around. I could tell they felt ripped off but they dared not admit it openly. They would probably share their disgust for the quieter moments, or for when they returned to wherever they came from. I guess they were still hoping that the 'eat as much as yu like food and drink' would compensate for their disillusionment.

Nearly everyone walked in the direction of the makeshift tables and chairs, to secure a place by sitting down, or by leaving a part of their belongings on the table, and then got up to fill their bamboo cups. There was a choice of rum punch, rum punch or rum punch. It was a 'drink-as-much-as-you-like-rum-punch' party.

I sat there, watching two men lay down smooth planks of wood which would soon constitute the 'dance-floor'. One thing I can say is that the people who were setting up the atmosphere for the evening, were very resourceful. Out of a few pieces of wood they had made a stage, a dance floor, tables and chairs and with the assistance of drapes and lighting they had transformed the beach into something almost magical.

It soon started getting dark, and we could no longer see the blemishes of moments before. Instead, we saw a white stretch of sand, calm clear water, coconut trees, people sitting at long tables with red tablecloths, drinking 'wine' out of sophisticated mugs.

The spotlight lit the stage, giving it a professional aura, and the band that had been criticized for their ragged attire, started singing melodious songs of well-known artists, creating a feeling of warmth and passion, negating the urge to criticize.

I didn't mind rum punch. Drinking it would help me feel less conspicuous. My light-headedness would eradicate any feelings of self-doubt or self-consciousness.

Another busload came, and there were some welcoming black faces on it. I saw a couple of women (unattached) and I felt a bit more relaxed. They came and sat at my table.

It wasn't long before the food was served (eat-as-much-as-you-like-until-it-done) and it was done one plate full! However, the entertainment had been selected to both please and entice. A good-looking, well-defined greased-covered (to enhance definition) man appeared, wearing a g-string. He was very provocative. The tourists were asked to "look anywhere", but anywhere they looked they had to put money there'. By the time he had finished, money was oozing out of his g-string, both at the front and at the back. I put $10 'there'.

A fire-eater performed - creating both tension and excitement; then limbo dancers appeared and encouraged participation. A lot of people joined in and then, to round it off, they had a competition – "who would be the most daring?". One of the tourists bared her breasts, another bared her thonged behind, a man exposed his ginger pubic hairs and another his tan-forsaken bum, all in an effort to win a bottle of white rum. The girl who bared her breasts won the competition.

It ended at 10.30 p.m.

IT'S THE CULTURE, NOTHING PERSONAL

The next day, I decided that I would take out my braids. It took me 4 hours to take all the braids out. I found out where a beauty salon was and made an appointment for them to cut and style my hair, and to give me a manicure and a pedicure.

I kept my appointment. I was attended to instantly (as there was nobody waiting) and shown a wooden stool to sit down on. I marvelled at their attentiveness. My feet were placed in a massage bowl immediately with warm suds, and a table was pulled up in front of me with all the systems in place for a manicure.

I was instructed to put my fingers in a little bowl containing creamy water, and I obeyed. Just as I did so, a good looking and well-groomed oriental-looking woman came into the shop and asked how long it would take to get a manicure.

"Immediately" the owner said.

She instructed the girl who was shaping my nails to attend the "Chinee" woman, as they were called then. Jamaica had a large population of indigenous Chinese. They were called the "money people" because the majority of them were merchants and property owners, so when they entered an establishment they commanded immediate respect without saying a word. The table was then whizzed from in front of me, leaving my dripping fingers suspended in animation. Contemptuous of protocol, the table was then calmly placed in front of the Chinese woman, whose projected butt nuzzled its way into a cushioned chair – a chair set-aside for 'special' clients.

I was dumbfounded. My swarthy countenance had again nullified my existence. I should have stood up and walked out, but my feet were immersed in water, and besides, the massage had a somewhat soothing effect on me. I just sat there mummified, acknowledging that it was not a business culture, it was nothing personal.

That manicurist believed someone should be treated differently based on the perception of his or her status,. I pacified myself – She didn't know better.

One screw face gyal, whose face favour bullfrog, continued where the other had left off. She was feeling resentful for some reason and I sensed her aggression when she started filing down my toenails. She tittered when I exhibited signs of uneasiness. She was so determined to extract a piece of dead skin lodged beneath my nail that she dug and wrenched at it until my toe bled. I wanted to push her off but I guess she was just trying to do her job properly. When she finally retrieved it, she showed it to me.

I do not know what incensed her to perform a pedicure without any effort to ease my discomfort. She put some iodine on the cut, causing me to flinch—it stung and despite the blood trickling down the side of my big toe, she continued to file down my toenails to a flat finish.

After a while, the other girl came back (the one who had been attending to the "Chinee") and she finished my pedicure. What a difference! The girl was so gentle. My tension subsided. My toenails were painted in a fluorescent orange and I asked for a French manicure, also. By the time they had finished with me, I was looking sharp!

The next day, I went to the Seagull as usual, but this time, as a reformed human being. They didn't even realise I was the same person. I suspected my anonymity when they brought me a menu instead of telling me what the 'special' was. Anyway, because they gave me so much attention, I gave the waiter a tip. I was feeling generous! I decided to visit a different beach (it was only JA$5 to get in).

I spread my towel out, and proceeded to lay down. I heard some voices:

"I have several gyal yu know, but only one h'ooman"

Then came the irritating hissing sound:

"Psst... psst" (someone was trying to capture my attention). "Excuse me, miss"

"Not, again.." I thought.

I looked up and saw someone smiling. He looked O.K. from a distance, but I couldn't see his face properly because I didn't have my contact lenses in. All I knew was that the voice came from amongst four men sitting on the lifeguard stand and I could only assume that it was the one 'skinning im teet' (as my mother would say).

"Do you mind if I come over and sit next to you?" I remembered the voice:

"Aren't you the one that just said that you have plenty of gyal but only one woman?

There was a jeer from the men. I had obviously made him feel shame.

"No, no... it wasn't me... well, yes, it was me, but its man talk.. I only have one woman."

"Oh, you only have one woman? and now you want to make it two? I ridiculed.

"I would like to talk to you, if I may?" he asked interrupting the sentence.

I noticed that his diction was pleasantly precise and the inflexion in his tone, well placed. He came over and stood next to me. He was attractive by comparison, clean-shaven. His shoes (I had to look at his shoes) passed the test—they were polished to a distinct sheen. His black trousers had a razor sharp seam. Hmmmm I thought, not bad.

"May I talk to you for a few minutes before I go on duty?"
"On duty?"

"I'm a police officer.. I am not on duty now.. but I will be in a few minutes"

(No wonder he looked so sharp! I thought).

"Yes, by all means, do..." I said moving over so he could share my towel.

A police officer? My mother had warned me about them. She told me they were promiscuous and that they would break your heart. I had never met a police officer before, apart from my father and my brothers, and even then, by the time I met them they were no longer in the police force. My father was the reason my mother hated policemen, and it was from her experience this warning stemmed. I was on holiday, a policeman, or any other man for that matter would not have the opportunity to break my heart, besides I only had three days left - what could happen in three days?

It was refreshing to speak to such an articulate and attractive individual. We spoke for a while, exchanged numbers and before he left to go on duty, he asked if he could bring me some ice cream later that evening.

Rebelling against my mother's advice: "of course.. I will look forward to it".

Auntie Sonia called me that evening and I told her about the event of the day. I was very excited. We arranged to see each other the following week.

TINGS A GWAAN

The second week was when everything started happening. I met Victoria, a middle-to-upper class English lady, of mixed parentage (her class seemed to matter) who had arrived with her two 'well-spoken' and well-bred sons, to Jamaica. Her husband had deferred their vacation so many times that she decided to leave without him. They had hired a bus for themselves for US$100 a day. It had fifteen seats and they had used it for sightseeing.

"If only we had met before, you could have come with us" she said sincerely.

"Well, I have run out of money now, anyway, but it was nice of you to ask". I told her that I was glad that I had given the hotel receptionist a US$100 deposit, because I would have money when I left the island.

"They tried to get the deposit from me, she responded, but I wouldn't give it to them. I told them that I wasn't going to make any phone calls."

"And they accepted that?"

"What could they do?

Maybe I should have been more assertive, too. But it didn't really occur to me to challenge them—I thought it was a ruling of the hotel. I also met two German women, (an aunt and her niece) who were at loggerheads with each other for economic and moral reasons. The aunt (Helga - still living in Germany and aged about 47 years) had a nice figure and wanted to show it off in a bikini, and stand naked by a window, while the niece felt it was inappropriate behaviour.

Helga was very friendly, however, her niece (Maria - now living in

California and aged about 34) felt that she was too old to wear a bikini and that it was immoral to stand naked before a window. Adopting a tourist mindset, Maria felt that Helga had to be careful: "you could be taken off and raped". Helga, was a frequent visitor to the Island, and was convinced that Maria's concern was unsubstantiated.

I couldn't help asking Maria about the deposit - she hadn't paid a deposit either. She had told them that she had only come with US$100 and there is no way in the world she was going to give it to them. I felt as though I had been gullible, and as long as I got it back, I didn't care, although, without a receipt, could I prove I gave it to them? I didn't let it worry me for too long – the policeman was coming around later.

The policeman brought around the grape-nut and cherry ice cream that evening. It tasted delicious. The evening was stimulating and I woke up feeling energised.

I met my Auntie Sonia the following day. I felt much better, things were falling into place. I picked up my book and started reading it again. I was in a calmer mood now.

MOSQUITO A GO KILL ME

Auntie Sonia picked me up from the Hotel. The first thing she warned me about was mosquitoes in her 'yard'. I had shown my hesitancy about going to her place but she had insisted.

"It's alright, she said "I will put out de ting fe kill dem, fih yu".

I took my long nightie with me, trousers, a long-sleeved blouse and a jacket - If necessary I would sleep with them on, even though it would mean overheating.

I had only been bitten twice so far, and I only had two days left to go before I left the island. It would be a pity to go and visit Auntie Sonia and come back with mosquito bites all over my skin.

"I don't travel with all dese people you know" (pointing to a line of disquieted and unseemly females) "they are too noysey and we haf to wait too lang." Her voice was verging towards arrogance. "I always charta a taxi."

"Charter a taxi?" I thought people only chartered planes, I quizzed.

"Oh, no, my dear, we charter taxis out here and it will cost me JD$60, but it drops me off right at my gate". She spoke with a twang.
We went around the corner and got into a 'taxi'. A beaten down piece of tin that rumbled along like it had stomach ache. Every so often we would be pitched from our seats as the driver swerved to avoid a large hole in the road or drove over a ditch that he did not see in time.

Auntie Sonia's apartment was on the top of a hill.

"I hope yuh skin don't like mosquitoes", she laughed.

We have plenty of dem up here but I have been here too long so dem don't bodder me"

I winced. Why did she have to remind me?

We had to walk up a long pathway past a bauxite field, and over some pipes before we reached her place. When we reached it, a grilled door prevented us from going inside. It was secured with a large padlock with a combination code. I had only seen combination padlocks used at the gym or on a safe. Immediately, I had a sense of foreboding - the presence of mosquitoes. The humidity was un-bearable, and already my body started itching. I kept hitting myself. I was paranoid.

As soon as we arrived, we caught up on old times and had quite a few laughs before resigning to bed. She turned out the light and it was pitch black. Not dark, pitch black. I couldn't see anything. I was in bed with my long nightie and my jacket. I had covered my head with the sheet and still through all this, I imagined the mosquitoes, bellicose in the unmerciful darkness.

I tried to free myself from imagined and real insects. I could not sleep. I was slapping my legs, neck and my arms, from insects that were not there, and missing those that were.

Morning could not come soon enough.. I jumped up at 6.00 with two red bumps—one on my shoulder, the other on my back. The mos-quitoes had successfully penetrated the silky barricade. Auntie Sonia had woken too, and was in the kitchen making breakfast (liver and breadfruit). I ate breakfast and watched her get dressed for work.

The phone rang.

"Hullo Stanley... what time will yu be ready?"

[He must have said 8 o'clock]

"O.K. I will be ready by 8.00".

Auntie Sonia looked at me. "That was my ride. I meet him down the road, him is a good-good frien'".

I looked at my watch. After having a shower, preparing breakfast and washing the leftover plates it was 7.30 a.m.

Auntie Sonia was combing her hair. She seemed to be taking an inordinate amount of time considering she had not put on her clothes yet, or eaten her breakfast. She was teasing her hair with the comb and pampering it where it didn't need it. Her hair looked perfect to me. It had been ten minutes, and it had reached a stage where stroking the petting did not seem to make any difference.

"Auntie Sonia! you should be putting on your clothes now.. it is 7.45 and you are supposed to meet Stanley at 8.00. Your hair looks fine." I affirmed.

"Top rush me man!"

I remained quiet. I didn't understand it. She was dependent on someone for a ride and she was just taking her time as though it didn't matter. Besides, which, she started work at 8.30 — if she missed the ride she would be late. It didn't occur to me that 'Stanley' was used to her lack of time management skills.

She lifted the hair spray and sprayed her coiffure.. then she dipped her fingers in some gel and patted it on the side. Took the sharp tail of the afro comb and drew designs on the side of her head. I couldn't believe she was doing all of this, while in her bra and panties, with 7 minutes left! But she was.

Finally satisfied, she put her blouse and skirt on and placed a multi-coloured scarf about her neck. Somehow the scarf didn't look right to her... she twisted it and spun it and took it off and put it back on, tried it one way and then another..

"Auntie Sonia! it's 8 o'clock".

"Hush man, yu making me nervous... I don't like to rush yu know".

"But you have someone waiting. You should allow yourself enough time".

For a moment I felt guilty, after all, she had got up early to make me breakfast, but she didn't have to spend so much time on her hair and her scarf – that was my point – especially when she was running late.

She seemed satisfied with her scarf at last, and then it came time for the belt. The belt was made for the skirt and seemed to match pretty well to me, but no, Auntie Sonia needed a contrast. So, rummaging in her wardrobe (8.09) she looks for an alternative, and finds another one to put on.

"He's probably gone by now," I mumbled, seeming more worried than she was.

"Me ready, man, me ready.. I don't even have time to eat my lobster. I'll have to take it with me." Unstressed, she found it appropriate to be humorous.
"When you come to America, Auntie Sonia, you will have to learn to be on time, otherwise you'll be without a job" I remarked, agitated.

"Yes, Myrna man, I will deal with that when I reach".

We walked out of the door, secured the grilled gate with the padlock, spun it to set the combination and walked towards Stanley's house, which was literally about two houses away. [I didn't realise he lived so close by – I felt a little silly].

"See. yu deh a rush me and de man don't even ready yet", she snapped forgetting to put on her speaksy spokesy accent.

It was true, he wasn't ready. So why give a time? He might as well have said, just come when you're ready. We didn't have a long wait though—maybe five minutes more, but that wasn't the point – it was now 8:20 a.m. I had agitated myself for nothing and had also succeeded in flustering Auntie Sonia.

BYAH DREAD

Winston called to say he would be at the hotel by 3.00 in the afternoon. I called the receptionist and advised her that I was expecting my nephew and that she should call me down when he arrived.

My nephew (on my mother's side, and who I didn't know very well at the time) arrived uncharacteristically on time for a Jamaican — 3.00 on the dot. The receptionist called me and I came down and met him. He was heavy laden with a big bag, forcing him to slouch over. I wondered if he planned to stay over.

"Are you hungry?" I asked him, a ruse to lure him from the hotel.

"I am sorry you couldn't come up to my room—visitors are not allowed in guest rooms" I continued.

"Me stay a dis hotel already yu know.." he said.

(I wasn't sure what he meant by that declaration and I wasn't really interested).

I had daily subsistence left of JA$220 left which was enough to treat him to lunch, provided I chose the meal.

"Yeh, mon, me starving"

"Well, I'm going to treat you a meal."

He didn't seem appreciative.

"Me need fe mek a phone call to someone pon dem cellular phone."

[Cellular Phone? that call will cost a bit].

I didn't respond.

"Bwoy me 'haffee get hole' of dis man fe mek a transaction."

"There is a phone in the Seagull, you can use that", I suggested.

We went in and I waited to be seated while Winston went to use the phone. Anticipating his choice, I ordered a vegetarian meal for JA$95.

He came back shortly:

"One bwoy deh pon de phone a talk him foolishness"

"Well, just hang around and wait—what would you like to drink?" I asked, hoping that he would say ice water):

"Mek I see de menu"
[Supposing he orders beer or something like that, I wouldn't have enough money].

"Jus get me some limeade"

Relieved, I knew I could afford that.

He went back to the phone and came back smiling. He had obviously made the connection:

"Me get hole of me frien'. Him tell me seh a session a gwan tonight a 'Dead En'. Yu wan' go?"

"I haven't been anywhere, so I might as well"

"Alright but me can't tek de bag wid me... me cyan leave it inna de 'otel room 'til later?"

"Yes, o.k." I said reluctantly.

We ate, I paid, and we left.

"Where do you want to go?" I said, showing no mercy for his burden.

"Tek de bag upstairs fe me na" he appealed.

I took it and lugged it to my room, I wondered what was in it as I dumped the heavy monstrosity on the floor.
I refreshed myself a little, put on some pants because I didn't want the mosquitoes biting my legs, changed my blouse, and returned.

"Mek we go up soh" he said pointing to the makeshift beach where some street urchins assembled.

Here we go, I thought, but followed him obediently. He stopped— he noticed someone he recognized:

"Wa'appen sah?"

"Rasta man - Wa'appen?"

"Me cool, mon.. irie, mon"

"So iz wah yu a seh?

"Me dyah, yu know.."

This unintelligible and invented vocabulary had them riveting in bouts of laughter for about fifteen minutes. I noticed that by accentuating the patois it transformed it into code language. It was the way they communicated when they didn't want a 'non-Jamaican' to understand what they were saying. I understood every word. I was pleased with myself, it qualified to my Jamaicanness.

Intermittently, Winston put a protective arm around the shoulders of his acquaintance and whispered something. Sporadically he would lift his head up, and twist it from side to side in a sinister fashion imitating an undercover agent. Occasionally, he would nod in my direction as if to confirm that everything was under control.
After about five minutes, I got fed up and told Winston I wanted to go.

Sensing my exclusion, he decided to introduce me to his 'bredren':

"A me niece dis" he boasted, as if he was taking credit for my cultivated appearance.

They both stood there approvingly nodding their heads.

Big deal, as if I needed their endorsement, I thought reproachfully.
"Yu smoke?" his 'bredren' asked.
"No, I don't", I responded shortly.

We walked off the roadside into a secluded spot and found ourselves tempting fate, vegetated on the edge of a cliff, overlooking the sea. The scenery was beautiful. The harsh environment was lost in its beauty and I looked out towards the skyline where nebulous buildings formed geometric faces within which, admonishing red lights flickered, like eyes squinting.

The sea silently brushed against the sand and recoiled spontaneously. A man and a woman passed, holding hands, laughing... I reminisced for a while.

How romantic. Her long hair was waving in the wind. I wanted to toss my braids in the breeze, while walking with that someone special but I was alone – physically and emotionally.

Meditative influences had been activated unconsciously. I had been involuntarily narcotised. I stopped reflecting on what I didn't have and appreciated the immediate beauty of my surroundings and what was accessible in the here and now. This camaraderie, this ability to see beauty; to feel peace; to understand and feel understood. I felt reconciled. My time was mine to do what I chose with it. I chose to be here overlooking a cliff—to be with my nephew as he consumed the billowing smoke that formed a cloud over his head.

I watched him remove his tam. His accusing dreadlocks slithered across his brown complexion like large pythons. If only I had a paint-brush!

After about fifteen minutes of meditation, silent musing, exchanging monosyllabic 'words of wisdom', we got up and started walking towards 'Dead En'.

"Me meet someone yu know - a Canadian - 'im a goh do a ting fe me" my nephew announced triumphantly.

"Really...?" I said, out of habit more than interest.

As we walked towards our destination, Winston stopped several times, conversing with questionable inhabitants.
"Wha'ppen. Byah-Dread?" ('Byah' was Winston's nickname).

"Me coool, mon, irie.. "

Off they would go whispering again, and the formulated dialogue would repeat itself like the rhyme of a song.

I started to become impatient. This was not a woman's scene. I was not that desperate to hear music... but I followed him as he liaised with his comrades, and I stopped when he stopped.

"So what flight yu a leave pon?" Winston turned to me and asked.

"Shrouder Airlines" I responded curiously, wondering what that could have to do with the person he was talking to.
"Where yu come aaaf, New York?

"No, Newark, why?"

"Me bredren here have a suitcase him want someone fe check in fe him, but him waant it fe goh a New York"

"Well it's just as well I am going to Newark then, isn't it?" I responded exasperatingly.
We walked in silence. Winston bought me a rum punch which I sipped it slowly (there were no restrooms). Every now and then he would leave me and talk with 'his bredren'. I kept drinking until I felt a bit tipsy, and then I started feeling tired, and then I started feeling out of place.

The squinting eyes in the scorched visage of a wandering beggar (no more than 5 or 6 years old) came up to me:

"Beg yu a two dol..."

Viciously amputating the sentence, I spat: "Don't beg!" and ruthlessly turned my back on what the natives called a 'slum youth'.

"Dem 'ave money yu know, more money dan me an' yu. Is dem mudda sen' dem out fe beg.." I heard somebody say as if trying to justify my hostility.

"Winston, I want to go back to the hotel" I said.

"O.K. I will see if I can get yu a lift" he said peacefully.

We started walking in the direction of the hotel when he met another one of his 'bredren' and asked him to drop me off at the hotel.

"Don't forget to come for yuh bag..." I reminded him. "...remember, Winston, I'm leaving first thing tomorrow morning"

"Naah, man, dat bag is h'important - me cyan't leave dat". A calm demeanor settled on him like satisfaction.

"What time does 'Dead En' finish? I enquired.

"H-h'it a g-gwaan til m-marnin'" came an unregulated utterance.

I got into the car, which looked like a mangled saucepan and drove as though it had no tyres and was dropped off at the hotel. If I had any sense I would have asked the guy to wait for the bag, but I didn't think about it until it was too late. The guy drove off. I was so exhausted, I fell asleep.

DE BAG LEF .. H'AN HIM GAAN

I woke up about 5.00 a.m. The bag was still there. "Oh No!" I exclaimed. I showered quickly and went downstairs and asked one of the guys at the desk if they thought "Dead En' was still going on. They said no, it would have finished about 2.30 a.m.

"But my nephew's bag is here!" I howled frantically, as if they could do anything about it.

Thank God I had a number for him. He had been staying in a hotel in Montego Bay and I wondered how he had booked into a hotel and not been relegated to the status of a tourist. I surmised that it was more than checking into a hotel that determined one's designation. I asked the operator to get the number for me. As it was so early in the morning, the operator got the number quickly. Someone picked up.

"Is Byah Dread there?" I asked, thinking I had better ask for him by his 'native' nom de plume.

"No, im call fe seh him gone a Salem wid two frien"
"When de he call?"
"Some time dis marnin'"
"Sometime this morning?" I repeated flabbergasted. [He could have called me at the same time].
"But his bag his here, he has left his bag here and I'm leaving this morning.. the hotel will not be responsible for it after I check out.. I don't know what to do?" Verbiage spewed out of my mouth uncontrollably.

I was angry and disoriented and marginally hysterical. How could he do this? He knew I was leaving! I could not fathom any excuse that could exonerate his behaviour. If he had the decency to inform his roommates that he was leaving to go to Salem, why couldn't he show me the same courtesy?

"So what am I supposed to do with it?"

"Bring it cum," a voice said calmly.
"Bring it cum? How much will it cost to bring it from Grosvenor Street to where you are?" I asked.

"About JD$5"

I had JA$200 in my purse... I would still have enough to buy breakfast when I got back. I asked for the address.

"I don't know de h'address yu know, de 'otel deh pon Top Road'

"Top Road? — what is that a name of a street?

"Naah, mon.." he said with a chuckle "jus tell dem seh a de road dat run on top o' de houses dem."

"A road that runs on top of the houses? How is the driver going to know where to go without a proper address?"

"'Im wih know, mon, 'im wih know.. truss me, man—jus' bring de bag come".

A man hailed down a taxi for me in about five minutes. I was relieved. The man was right. He did know exactly where to go with minimal code word instructions. Without the name of the road, without the number of a street, with a signpost, they could find their way to a destination by land marking in their own language. I was amazed at the method of communication.

It was now 6.15 a.m and we arrived outside the hotel within around

10 minutes. I went inside the hotel and put the bag on the floor. "This is for room 8909" I told them, and immediately made a motion to exit the hotel.

"No, yu can't leave it deh so, yu 'ave to wait til someone come h'an pick it up—supposing dem don' colleck h'it?"

"But I just spoke to someone a little while ago, they know it is coming.."

He ignored me and made the phone call:

"Sambaddy has jus deliver a bag 'ere, would yu like fe come dung and accep ih?"

I assumed the answer was in the affirmative. I confirmed it and it was so. I turned to leave not wishing to meet any more of Winston's 'bredren'. The driver was doing something with his spark plugs. When he saw me he got back into the car and we were back in the hotel within 15 minutes.

The return drive gave me time to think. I understood now why Winston was in Jamaica. Only his fellow natives would tolerate his behaviour. America should have hardened me, but it hadn't. I should have made him lugga-lugga with his bag instead of offering to look after it for him. I should have made him walk all the way to 'Dead En' with it!I realised at this point that notwithstanding the majority of Jamaicans are punctual, polite and considerate, I would find it difficult to live in the undisciplined culture that Winston had aspired to.

Order, punctuality, integrity were important to me, but these traits were not taken seriously by the people I had interacted with on this journey. I deduced that time was both irrelevant, irreverent and relative in the Jamaican culture. To say "I will be dere in a couple hours well" could range between 2 and 24 hours! Time was a critical anomaly. To say "I am coming over later", and not turn up at all, wasn't considered a breach of etiquette. I was brought back to the present:

"Dat will be $140.." he said, glowering, with an outstretched palm. "$140? but it wasn't even 5 minutes away?" I responded. [He must have meant $5 U.S!] "$140 he repeated! He wasn't grinning anymore". I gave him the $200 and he put it all away. I waited: "My change please?"

The audacity of him - apart from overcharging me, he expected a tip as well?

TEK YUH TIME MON..

No money to buy breakfast, but I had peace of mind now, and besides, I had my security deposit to collect. I could retrieve it and buy
breakfast. I still had enough time. It was 6.45 and my driver was not
due until 7.50. I decided to check out. I needed my US$100 re-
turned.

I approached the desk but someone else had just started checking
out before me, so I had to wait. It took about twenty minutes before
I finally got attended to.

The man turned on the computer to work out my hotel bill. "There
is a JA$53 charge outstanding for phone calls, ma'am." (I had worked
it out to be JA$94 but I wasn't going to say anything).

"I understood that the phone calls would be taken out of the deposit"

"Oh, so yu 'ave a deposit here, ma'am?"

"Yes, US$100! and I need it now so I can buy my breakfast and check
out. It wasn't even recorded that I had left a deposit and I didn't
even have a receipt to prove that I had paid it. My US$100 was left
to the integrity of management and the honesty of its staff.

He obviously found my predicament amusing, and started smiling.
"Well, we 'ave a problem here yu know, yu 'ave fe wait until de girl
come wid de key, an' she don't come until 7.00 dis marnin'"

[I was wishing I could wipe that grin off his face...]

"With what key?"

"The key fit de safe"

"Look, my transportation will be here soon, I want my money now.. they were quick enough to take it, now I want it back." Rage had matured because of the culmination of incidents that had transpired during the last 14 hours.

"Go 'ave some breakfast mon, and by de time yu finish de girl should be here" he interrupted, undisturbed by my relative hysteria.

"I don't have any money!" I hissed acrimoniously. "You have my money in your safe!"

"Well, mi cyan't give it to yu because mi don' 'ave de key, ma'am, yu will 'ave to wait until one of de girls come.." [don't you bloody ma'am me, I muttered] .

"But it is 7.00 now and they are not here."

"Dem soon come.. ma'am, dem soon come". ["soon come" was relative and had no intrinsic value].

I started rummaging in my bag to see if any money had been discarded somewhere, and found US$5. Well at least I could get some breakfast.

"See how de good Lord shine 'im merciful light pon yu ma'am, go get some breakfast now ma'am" he entreated.

This ma'am, ma'am business, was getting on my nerves now, and sounded patronising! Mocking my sensitivities, but there was nothing I could do. I had reneged control. I was on unfamiliar territory and could no longer identify with a breed that I could only term as flippant. I reinstated my British 'values'.

I went into the restaurant which was meant to be open at 7.00 a.m. It had just past 7 o'clock and the ladies were putting out the napkins, knives and forks and putting glasses of ice water on the table. [This should have been done already].

A young lady approached me and I told her I was checking out of the hotel in 30 minutes. It was now 7.15 and I wondered if she could bring me the 'special' whatever it was, as quickly as possible.

"Yes" she said, "The special is Corned beef hash with green bananas".

["Look I don't care what it is, just go and get it!" I felt like saying!]

"Yes, yes, now quickly, pleease!"

Something about the culture provoked agitation. Something about re-iteration and futile definitions incensed me. I was on shaky ground. I yearned for stability of 'home', for order. Even ordering food seemed chaotic and made, what could have been a satisfying experience, a stressful one. Maybe I needed to lighten up, but somehow I couldn't.

She went over to another table and finished putting down the remaining knives and forks that she had in her hand. Then she started straightening the napkins. "Quee-yuh!" Did she not hear me say that I was checking out of the hotel in 30 minutes? She wouldn't even turn around so I could catch her eye and give her one look! She just edged her marga self around the tables and retreated around the back. "mek she gwaan" I mumbled in my British-patois.

It was 7.30 and I had not received my plate of food yet. I was getting so flustered — she administered each task so slowly, it was unbelievable. I saw her come out. On noticing my threatening expression she disappeared behind a partition. About two minutes later she came out with my plate.

I was ungrateful by this time.

"Have you got any hot pepper?" My manners had got lost somewhere between irritation and disappointment.

"Yes ma'am"

"Well, go get some fih me, nah" I ordered.

Deciding I would probably have to wait fifteen minutes before the pepper arrived, I started eating my breakfast without it; drinking my coffee and sipping my orange alternately. However, she brought the pepper relatively quickly (I had only eaten one green banana and a quarter of my fried dumpling) so I tipped some onto the remainder of my breakfast.

It was the first time I had not enjoyed my breakfast since arriving on the island and in my anxiety I was eating it too fast. Someone shouted over the tannoy.

"Is Ms. Loy here?" I put the last morsel in my mouth and ran to the reception desk. It was 7.35 and the girls had not arrived yet.

"Are yu Ms Loy?" [still munching] I nodded.

"Yuh driver is here to take yu to the airport".

"Where's my money?" I demanded.

The desk clerk reacted.

He called someone to ascertain the whereabouts of the key to the safe.

"The girls should 'ave been here by 7.00", he said, trying to pacify me.

"Look if your hotel does not trust its staff, then it should not employ them", I snapped.

It was now 7.45 a.m. My transportation had arrived five minutes early. Just as he seemed to get the information, one of the girls came in and handed the key casually to him. He asked me for the $JA53 for the phone calls, which I had from the change the taxi driver gave me and gave me back the whole deposit of US$100 (He forgot to deduct the US$20 for the security box).

Justice had been served. I felt much better. Without a word of indebtedness, I struggled with my hand luggage to the door, my large suitcase having already been taken outside.

BOGUS PASSPORT?

The driver loaded my luggage on and drove me to Sangster Airport in Montego Bay, where I checked in my suitcase. While waiting to board the plane, I bought 3 bottles of white rum and a book of award winning Jamaican stories. I went upstairs to wait for the plane. I was still feeling a little agitated and just wanted to get home. Things had not gone well since the 'bag' incident. The plane left on schedule and we arrived at Miami 11.00. For 2.5 hours I waited to get through the customs and immigration procedures.

Finally, it was my turn. The inspector looked at me suspiciously. He looked at me and then at the photograph several times. (Of course the photograph doesn't look like me, you berk, I have glasses on, and my braids have been taken out). I took off my glasses but he didn't look up. He started trying to defile my passport by pinching at the corners of the front page. Then he started looking over his shoulders as if he wanted someone to call security. I definitely did not need this.

I looked at the clock, I was running out of time and patience. It had been rumoured that illegal immigrants used bogus passports to gain access into America. They would come to Miami and then because a passport was not required from Miami to New York, they would use other means to get there. But surely the inspector could differentiate a forgery from the real thing? Obviously he could not because he was just about to desecrate the protective covering that secured my photograph when he decided to check my visa status.

"G4 visa, eh?, Secretariat. So you work for the Government?" he asked. [So the G4 visa is what determines whether a passport is valid or a forgery?]

"You have a good job — does it pay well?"

I ignored him. He twitched nervously.

"Do you like working there?" he said, trying to humour me.

I turned my head as though I hadn't heard him and looked to see how many poor buggers were waiting in line. There were hundreds of them. If this moron was the one inspecting all the passports, they would be here until midnight.

"Tear it up now, na.. tear it up if yu bad" My British-patois resounded in my head. Did it actually make a difference that I was a Government official? This was ludicrous, these agents did not have a clue how to differentiate a forgery from the real thing. He let me go through based on my status.

I scowled, snatched my passport and strutted like an ostrich towards the carousel.
With 20 minutes left to board the plane, I had to find the carousel my luggage was placed on, retrieve it and check it in. I located my suitcase, picked it up and dragged it to the representative who told me to "Give it to the sky captain".

There were about six 'sky-captains'. I didn't know which one to give it to. I gave it to the one that approached me (assuming she had magically indicated to him in some way that he should take my case) and made my way toward the plane with twelve minutes left.

It seemed as though I was walking for miles. It was a good ten minutes walk to the plane and that was at a hurried pace. When I finally arrived, there was a line. The computer was down.

"People with boarding passes can get on the plane. the plane will be leaving in three minutes. "There had been no procedure whereby boarding passes had been dispensed. The procedure was ad hoc. Trying to get the attention of the airline representatives was near impossible. So I just boarded the plane and took out my ticket. Luckily, I had one of those tickets that has the boarding pass attached to it. I did not need a separate boarding pass.

It wasn't until I boarded the plane that I realized the carton with the rum was missing. Somewhere amidst this confusion the three bottles of rum I had bought, were misplaced. My uneasiness mounted. I don't think it was mislaying the rum that caused the uneasiness but the culmination of events and non-events that had happened throughout the 2-week duration.

The plane landed at 5 o'clock on schedule. I disembarked at Newark, and waited for two hours until the blue light flickered showing no more baggage. My suitcase was not there—and no rum to drown my sorrows.

I put a claim in for my lost luggage at the office located in the airport. By the time they finished processing the application it was 8 p.m. I took a bus to Penn Station (since I didn't have any suitcases) and then decided to transfer to the bus that stopped right outside my building. I saw it coming, I picked up my hand-luggage, waited for it to stop but it sailed past my flailing hand, right passed me... what more could go wrong? They said bad things come in threes, they don't.

By the time I got to the my apartment, it was 9.30 pm. I pushed my key through the lock imagining the worst. However, I could still smell the sweet scent of pine I had administered before I left for Jamaica to deter potential cockroaches that may have wanted to occupy my apartment in my absence.

I walked towards my phone and listened to my messages—my usual callers. I flung my hand luggage on the floor, went into the kitchen and looked in the fridge. Took out a bottle of juice and raised it to my mouth swallowing greedily (why bother with etiquette?). I went back into my bedroom and I lay prostrate on the bed: 'home' at last.

I realised at that point that my home wasn't a place. It didn't matter whether I was living in Jamaica, America or Britain; home for me was where I felt comfortable. My home, therefore, was transportable.

It would be fair to say that I did not feel comfortable throughout the whole 2-week duration in Jamaica but there again, there were times I did not feel comfortable in the States either, or in England for that matter, but there were treasured moments where I enjoyed being part of an identifiable language and where the culture felt akin to my diverse personalities.

Jamaica is the home of many people who (although foreigners) have adapted well to the culture and traditions and who are so enamoured by the food, the music and the lifestyle that they have learned to overlook the lack of regime and order that was so important to me at that time.

10 yrs
LATER

Space and Identity.

It was now June 2003 (10 years after my return from the trip to Jamaica), I, as part of the 0,1 Space & Identity Team, had been given an opportunity to re-visit Jamaica to evaluate my miscellaneous identity and feelings of dislocation. I wanted to know if, like me, people of dual culture born in Britain, experienced feelings of estrangement when they visited the home of their parents, as I had.

This visit to Jamaica would enable me to compare previous experiences and analyse why I had felt so affected by the culture and the people a few years ago, and what impact (if any) my parents' influence had on my reaction to the Jamaican culture.

The Flight

The dual-journey could have started from several places, but my journey starts once again, at the airport.
After getting the ticket and ensuring I had an aisle seat, I started walking the route to the gates. As I crossed one bureaucratic hurdle after another I looked at my watch to see what time it was – it was 17:20hr, the plane was scheduled to leave at 17:40h. There was a group of us going, each with our own work-plan. We engaged briefly, I then went over to the phone booth to call my daughter when the tone of a grey-haired white lady calling Jamaica, caught my attention. It was obvious that she wanted everyone in close proximity to know she had someone to put her begonias out on the patio. It also seemed important to her that everyone in earshot should know that she was ordering her staff to clean the house and that her room was ready for her arrival: "Make sure there are fresh flowers in every room.. and has Hetty finished the ironing? "Has Garston swept the porch?" After the distraction, it was too late for me to make my call—The airline was boarding passengers.

I checked the seat numbering on the ticket and noticed that a young mixed-race woman and her son were occupying my seat. Attired in a candy-striped dress with a split that extended the length of her thigh, she sprawled out comfortably across the length of both seats. Her shoes were off, her bags were scattered around her, and her son was standing on the seat.

"Excuse me…" I said in a polite tone "..but you are occupying my seat". One eye cocked, the gyration of her neck, an animated wave of the hand indicated, that this was a woman with an attitude. Her obtrusive behaviour ignited frustration.

"I am not being separated from my son and his seat is over there", she said pointing with an indented forefinger in a direction I did not acknowledge. I remained silent for a few seconds which seemed like several minutes to see if she was making any effort to move but she wasn't. I repeated "Excuse me, but that is my seat you are sitting in". She turned her head towards the window and seemed deter-mined to hold the seat hostage

"I am extremely sorry that you are being inconvenienced" I continued calmly "…but I specifically asked for an aisle seat as I need the leg room". She turned back at me with a toss of the head. She opened her eyes defiantly as if to intimidate me and pointed to an area on the other side of the plane, the indication being that I should take the seat her son had been designated. I noticed a large mole by the side of her ear with two hairs protruding from it. I wanted to pull them out with blunt tweezers!

I couldn't get out of the aisle into my seat because her bags were in the way and her negotiating skills were falling on deaf ears. A line of agitated passengers had accrued which engaged the attention of the flight attendant.

"Is there a problem here ma'am?" she asked in an eloquent tone. I told her that either the lady or her child was occupying my seat, I didn't know which one. The stewardess looked at me as though I was being unreasonable. She gave me that: "Come-on, don't-be-difficult-lady-you are single you can sit anywhere.." kind of look. Had I been twenty years younger I might have been emotionally blackmailed into giving up my seat, but I wasn't 20 years younger so I didn't see why I should. I didn't like the attitude of the young lady, nor the behaviour of her spoilt child who was now clambering uncontrollably over the headrest onto the seat behind. As far as I was concerned, had she bought the ticket for her son instead of getting a free seat because he was under age, she could have arranged for her son to sit with her. I was adamant.

I had requested this particular seat and as far as I was concerned, the young lady, her son and her baggage could find somewhere else to sit! The exasperated attendant told her that it was at the discretion of each passenger whether or not they were prepared to relinquish their seats to accommodate other passengers and it seemed that in this instance, I had decided to abide by my right to retain the seat I had been designated. She reassured her that she would arrange for someone to swap seats to enable her to sit with her son and went. An acrimonious glare followed.

"Don't worry son..." (she remarked more loudly than was necessary) "I know you like looking out of the window.. but we have to move because this old bag won't let us sit here" she hissed rolling her marble-like eyes up at me. Her son started screaming (I think she pinched him to elicit sympathy) because it seemed a rather unnatural and sudden response to me. She could pinch him likkle more as far as I was concerned! I absorbed her glare as she snapped up her belongings and shuffled to an adjacent seat where she could sit with her son. I positioned myself comfortably in the seat. It really was a good seat — plenty of legroom. I was constantly acknowledging just how precious my personal space was to me.

The lady who had swapped with the young girl, was an elderly person in her mid 60's probably, and quite overweight. As I was putting my hand luggage in the overhead compartment, she squeezed herself into the window seat, her cotton covered rolls of flesh overlapping on each side. Instinctively, I told her that she was occupying my seat completely forgetting that I had requested the aisle seat: "If me did know dat me wasn' goin' get de window seat... me woulda never gi up me udda seat!" she lamented.

I was too embarrassed after she had moved her stuff over, to tell her I had made a mistake and that she could move back, so instead I suffered the imposition of her dominating my armrest and the various gradations of sounds that came from her mouth. She was soliloquising (this was all I needed). She had been staying in London for 6 months and now it was time for her to return to Jamaica before her visa expired. She was returning reluctantly leaving her pickney dem behind: "dem no really want me here yu know (she groaned).. Me know seh dem don't really want me 'ere.. yu waan see how quick dem carry me go a airport h'an drap me aaaf.. early-early. Dem couldn't h'even walk me to de plane.. dem just drap me h'aaf like luggage.. but h'it awright... h'it awright!" .

I could tell it wasn't alright, and that she was feeling hurt and rejected but she was trying to disguise her trepidation with a belligerent tone.I realised at this point that my concern was not just about personal space, but about my physical space as well.

This woman had become invasive—hissing, moaning.. shoving and grunting – she was encroaching on my space. She took a fruit out of a noisy plastic bag. Dissatisfied with its lacklustre she rubbed the fruit with its rasping container. It reminded me of someone opening a crisp packet or chomping popcorn in a cinema. I didn't recognise the fruit but whatever it was she banged it determinably against her teeth, gouged out a piece, examined the violated fruit and cupped the remainder in her lap.

While she ate the portion she had in her mouth, she stared straight ahead as though she was worrying about something. This process repeated itself until she had devoured all of it. The assortment of noises was overbearing—from the sound of gouging fruit; juice splashing against the insides of her mouth; the loudspeaker introducing the crew; people shuffling; children screaming or crying to general cordial chatter—I wondered when I could enjoy some silence. It was out of my control—sharing brought with it, compromise.

I diffused the sound with my earplugs and tried to sleep. However, the woman nudged me every time the attendant passed with the drinks trolley, or with the food: "Yu waan drink anyting? Yu waan't someting fe h'eat?" She was trying to be helpful but I found her intrusiveness irritating. I sat up and decided to drink some tonic water and eat some crackers. She didn't have anything to eat or drink she simply resumed her stance of staring into mid-air after she had meddled with my sanity. The flight was long and tiring and as I dipped in an out of sleep, I surrendered to my plight. We landed in Kingston 10 hours later.

The Arrival

The plane ride was long and not very comfortable. Unable to catch a substantive nap, I prayed simple to land safely and smoothly and my prayer had been answered. We arrived at Sangster Airport around 9:20 at night. There was no artificial lighting, only a wide open space. A few silhouettes betraying men who were standing surreptitiously against a wall which was illuminated by the runway lights.

Three sets of curved steps protruded from the plane forming long ladders on the tarmac. I smiled widely. I was in Jamaica. I took this moment to reclaim this new space and embrace the heavy air before going into the airport. It was strange coming out of the plane into the open air as opposed to the exit leading into an airport. Behind the aircraft stood the airport—an encased building, synonymous with bureaucracy. A sense of freedom was felt from being outside and unbound but I sensed restriction loomed inside the building where I had to go to have my passport stamped, handover my immigration papers and collect my luggage. The baggage came remarkably quickly, eradicating any suspicions that my luggage may have been tampered with.

I was continuously conscious of the reason for being in Jamaica this time. I searched inquisitively at each aspect that might dictate my perception of the people, the culture and the island. I looked tiredly at the representatives of hotels holding up name cards of the groups or person(s) that had been instructed to collect passengers but our group's name was not visible on any of the plaques. An airport helper came over to us with a trolley asking if we needed assistance. Each of us had brought luggage of a manageable size so assistance was not required—the man hissed his teeth and walked off.

We looked at each other, shrugged our shoulders and smiled. Tourism had begun. I noticed that the airport helper stood in eye shot of us as if he was hoping that we would fall over our luggage or something so he could gloat. His lips were pursed with vexation, but as soon as a traveller, disabled by the amount of luggage she had in tow was able to utilise his service, he immediately transformed his scowl into a friendly smile. He had been given the opportunity now to earn a living with dignity [no thanks to us!].

We went over to the desk to enquire about the transportation. The desk clerk picked up the phone, dialled a number and spoke very quietly to the person on the other end. After replacing the receiver he said that our transport was outside. I applauded the Magnolia Gardens Hotel for keeping their promise. We followed the clerk outside towards a tour guide coach. Our bags were loaded on the coach through the back window and after that was done the clerk whispered "Money matters.. money matters.."

At first we thought he wanted a tip for showing us to the coach, until we realised that Magnolia Gardens had simply directed the airport representative to put us on the coach at the cost of US$20 each! We couldn't argue, we were on our way.

The coach stopped at various hotels on the way. I was so tired, I dozed off until the driver shouted " Palm Leaves Hotel" which woke me up. The Magnolia Gardens wasn't too far away.

Shortly after the disturbance, we arrived via a bumpy pebbled road to the white luminescent front of a very large hotel, its gazebo beleaguered by mosquitoes. First impressions can be impactful, but there again, first impressions depend on one's state of mind at the time. Florescent lighting gave the hotel a panoramic feel. There was a swimming pool filled with what looked like, turquoise water. I noticed white wicker deckchairs partially obscured by large green plants. Inside, the ceiling was glittery. Specs of glass had been embedded into the ceiling making it sparkle.

The reception area spacious and clean – a rendezvous for affluent locals. This hotel was only hotel available at short notice. The receptionist offered us a cup of tea and a bit of toast at 11 o'clock at night – what service!! Shortly afterwards she showed us to our rooms. 'My' room was enormous. It was air conditioned, housed a dressing room area; kitchen; bathroom; cable TV and a phone. What more could a tired woman ask for? I had arrived safely after 15 hours and this was my room - my space. I had one thing to do before I settled down for the night which was to call my daughter to let know that I had arrived safe so that she could inform the rest of my family.

A decade down the line, the telephone service had to have improved. I went to the reception area and asked how I could make a call. I recalled a few years ago that the reception offered a service whereby each room had a phone line after you paid a deposit. I suspected that a hotel of this size would be equipped with credit card facilities and assumed I could pick up the phone, dial the number and it would be recorded as a debit. However, in this particular hotel, the receptionist was my only port of call if I wanted to make an international call and she was leaving for the night. I expressed how important it was for me to make the call. The former hospitality displayed by her was now replaced with frustration.

I didn't realise at the time that they closed the reception area at 11:00 p.m; nor did I realise that the receptionist had stayed 20 minutes late to welcome us; nor did I realise that they didn't accept credit cards (and I had irresponsibly left my mobile in the UK because I didn't want to incur unnecessary roaming charges) nor that the receptionist had to make each and every call. [No wonder hotel rooms were still available!] Reluctantly, the receptionist made the call to my daughter and I left a message for her since it was around 5:00 in the morning. The receptionist told me to leave a deposit of US$20 for the call, which I did and thanked her for making the sacrifice.

I took this opportunity to ask her what time breakfast would be served and she said 8:15 a.m. I told her I would make the call the following morning. I went back into my room and opened up my case marvelling at the amount of space I could enjoy. I peaked out of the window which boasted a veranda and a white wicker lounge chair. The swimming pool shimmered under the moonlight. I wish I could swim I thought. I returned to the job at hand, tired, but I needed to hang up my clothes. The wardrobe housed two mangled wiry atrocities hung in a disabled fashion on the rail. I revisited reception just in time to catch the receptionist before she left. "Can I have some clothes hangers please?" She huffed, glared at me in irritation, put down her bag and went around the back and handed over some hangers of similar distortion. "These are the only racks5 we have" I took them gratefully empathising with her attitude – it was late, she had been delayed from going home and she would have to walk to her destination and goodness knows how far that was.

I went back into my room and turned on the TV. For some reason I imagined Jamaica having her own TV stations. I was yearning to find an element in Jamaica that I could identify with but I continuously struck stalemate. I was quite disappointed to see the same channels on the TV in Jamaica as seen in the UK. I guess local channels were as expensive to run in Jamaica as they were in England. I coated my skin with mosquito repellent; it was past midnight—the air-conditioning kept the room cool, the sheets were crisp, I slipped between them and fell asleep.

Time – a matter of fact, not principle?

The ensuing days were as consciously absorbed as the first. I got up early the following morning to see if I could make a call. There was no-one at the reception desk. It was 7:00 a.m. I went back to my room. I looked out the window and saw the rest of the team by the poolside. They were a welcome sight. Familiarity in a strange setting was always welcome. I went out to join them. We were all hungry. The time in England was 1:00 in the morning and we hadn't eaten since the night before (except for a bit of dry toast [– yes it was dry now—the appreciation had worn off!) We still had an hour to wait for our traditional Jamaican breakfast and that had to be worth waiting for. There was something familiar with the way I was feeling now, and the way I felt back then, but I couldn't put my finger on it.

The receptionist called me inside. She had one of those grins that spanned the whole of the lower part of her face – a grin that indicated that she was glad to be alive. I had a call. It was my daughter. We spoke for a while and then I returned to the breakfast table—the breakfast had still not been served. It was now 8:20 a.m. We all, being conditioned to the British code of ethics, looked at our watches.

Punctuality prevailed even as tourists! We were counting the minutes. "Watch pot never boil" my mother used to say and experience warned me that the concept of time in Jamaica, was a matter of fact, not principle. "H'everyting cool mon". We all sat around the table prepared for us, which was in a gazebo type structure. We were the only ones at breakfast. "I wonder where everyone else is?" I remember remarking. The question remained unanswered.

The lady who was serving us introduced herself as Miss Bennett. She looked very young and had a pleasant voice. She had a wide mouth and inquisitive eyes. Her brown skin licensed her to be familiar. Her over-zealousness to help, seemed to have a manipulative quality.

"My name is Miss Bennett... I am here to serve you and I will be serving you throughout the duration of your stay. If you have any problems, please do not hesitate to let me know and I will do my best to help you. If I cannot help you, then I will find someone who will. I hope you have an enjoyable stay and I hope you enjoy your breakfast this morning".

She sounded like a pilot making an announcement over a tannoy just as he is about to take off. I have never known so many words to come out all in one sentence. The group were amused by her proficiency, they found her manner relaxing. I guess I needed to relax and not analyse things so much—but, there again, that was why I was in Jamaica this time around—to analyse, interpret, observe, internalise and identify with. I had been given creative licence for this exercise.

The breakfast came. Scrambled egg and toasted hardo bread. The Jamaican in me wanted to say: "a wah dis?" I was not sure if anyone, other than a British-Jamaican could identity with my disappointment. I had waited for hours for my first 'Jamaican' breakfast—a breakfast which was meant to be akin to my culture but which had ironically reacquainted me with being British. I might as well have stayed in England! Jamaica had become so disappointingly westernised. English television channels; scrambled egg, tea bags, what next?

As we sat there, a couple from a neighbouring town came in and sat down behind us. I had overheard them talking to the receptionist the night before. They were sitting for a while smiling and laughing. The woman had a glimmer of satisfaction on her face; they had obviously spent the evening together.

The gentleman was big set and had his back to me. Both were well-dressed and well groomed. I watched Miss Bennett bring them over a plate of ackee and saltfish and what looked like dumpling and bananas on the side, from where I was sitting. Walking past under the premise of getting something on the other side of the gazebo, my suspicions were confirmed.

I went back quickly and sat down. What was this? Favouritism? I didn't see a menu – there was no indication I had a choice. My mouth dropped open. I wanted to instigate a revolt. "Look at what they are eating" I whispered rather loudly if that is possible. "I am going to complain!" With an air of importance, I strutted inside and asked why we had been served scrambled eggs while the other couple clearly had ackee and saltfish?

"You didn't ask for it ma'am" was her soft reply.

"I didn't know I had to..." I responded rather defensively "..is there a menu?"
"No, Ma'am", she said.
"So how am I supposed to know what is available?" I retorted.
"By asking, ma'am".
"But supposing you don't have what I am asking for?" I said in a somewhat frustrated tone.
"Well then, ma'am, you won't be able to get it, you will have to choose something else." Her serenity was consistent.

I was confused. Will you please put an order in for me for tomorrow then, I snapped.

She looked at me puzzled and passed me a piece of paper she tore off from her notebook.

"Will you please write down what you want on that piece of paper". The piece of paper I was supposed to write on was the size of a sea shell, I was sure she would lose it, or would not understand my writing, so I went into my room, got a larger bit of writing and wrote on it..
"ACKEE, SALTFISH AND DUMPLING EVERY DAY PLEASE". That should give them the message.

I went back to the breakfast table and told the team that if we wanted ackee and saltfish, we would have to order it the night before.
A taxi which had been ordered by the receptionist, showed up to take us to Dunns River Falls and as it is when one first arrives on a hot Caribbean island, tourists tend to be enamoured by the service they receive. I was no different although I did not like to think that the attention was a privilege bequeathed to tourists only.

We went outside and realised that we couldn't all fit in the car—the car was designed to carry three in the back and one in the front (apart from the driver) and there were five of us. We related the situation to the receptionist who said that normally four people squeezed in the back and couldn't we try? Well, given that it was humid and the car did not have air-conditioning we opted not to negotiate and decided to wait for another car which turned up around 15 minutes later. I was muttering under my breath as to how she expected us to hitch up in one degay-degay car in such conditions?

Dunns River was only a couple of miles down the road, and the taxi driver gave us his number and told us to call him when we were ready. We told him that we would be ready in a couple of hours, but he told us to call him just in case we wanted to stay longer or leave earlier. He hadn't taken any money from us, so it seemed OK.

There wasn't much to do at Dunns River Falls after the novelty of getting into the water, participating with other like-minded tourists and eating variations of local fruit had worn off. Even though I had my swimming costume on underneath my sarong, I was too frightened to go near the falls. We all stood timidly on the edge of the falls long enough to take photographs, each of us reluctant to brave the menacing downpour.

The beach was quite empty so there wasn't much stimuli. We had been there about 20-30 minutes just enough time to eat the pattie, look around and decide that there had to be something more stimulating to do. We decided to all the taxi driver who had left us his number to pick us up, but kept getting voicemail. We left several messages and after waiting a further 30 minutes we decided to take another cab. We assumed the driver would turn up at the hotel to get his cab fare since he didn't take any money from us when he dropped us off but he didn't.

We took the taxi into the town centre and decided to find a Jerk Centre. We were guided purely by instinct and memory. We had seen the name of the Jerk Centre advertised in the hotel, so we asked a shoeless gentleman with cracked feet if he knew where the Jerk Centre was.

He grinned broadly (glad to be of service) opening a gappy mouth that vaguely resembled a double six! His feet were white from the seawater. You could tell how tough they were just by the way the bottom protruded out backwards beyond his Achilles heel. He spoke with some distortion and in a manner that was pleasing. He began describing the various roads, trees and buildings as he strode ahead of us, gesticulating as he explained the whys and wherefores along the way. After walking about ten minutes, we could see the Jerk Centre ahead. "We are alright now—we know where it is" one of us said.

The man looked at us and continued his 'tour-guide' role. Emphasis was needed in the form of some raw patois to get our point across. "Gwaan mon, we awright now" scowled a male member of the group, but the British patois didn't cut it, instead it sounded feeble and unconvincing. Our 'tour-guide' pointed to the tree describing what type it was and what season it flowered, and what type of leaves it produced. He then pointed out towards the hills "Jagga live up dere yu know," and mentioned a couple of other not so familiar celebrities who had chosen Jamaica for their holiday home. He was no longer concerned about our needs, he had an ulterior motive.

He proceeded to pick up a shell from the ground, revealing an embarrassing rip in the underside of his trousers. I could see his bare skin through it and what looked like unattractive scar tissue. He informed us that what he had picked up was the remnants of an almond, information that hardly contained value. He then informed us that there was a free 'Sunfest' "at Music Village". My ears pricked up at the words "Sunfest" "free;" now that was information of value. I said "what? Here in Ocho Rios?" "Yes, he confirmed, "h'it wi start arown mid-day". That was all I needed to hear—I had visions of famous artists performing – we would definitely go there in the afternoon.

Our 'tour guide' was with us for the duration. When we arrived at the Jerk centre, he proudly walked over to a table and started pulling out chairs for us to sit on. I was startled by someone shouting. He was being spurned by the proprietor:

"Get out... Get out dutty bwoy! Yu have no right whatsoever to be inside here!"

The man stood there unperturbed by the insult. Instead he stretched out his palm towards us seeking compensation for his service. He had walked a good way with us, showing us the sights, and bringing us to the jerk centre. He needed to be rewarded. I reached into my bag, but was interrupted by the irrational behaviour of the owner.

"Me seh, come out!" the owner of the centre shouted. I saw him hiss his teeth and dash towards the bar as if he was going to get something to beat him with. I could here him seh.. cha.. cha.. mek me fine... "

The man's eyes were beseeching. I continued looking in my bag for some change but I only had US20 bills. Anyway, the man didn't get a chance to be compensated. The owner of the shop came back with a big stick.. "get out dutty bwoy.. I don't want yuh backside inside here!"
The shoeless man was forced to run, revealing a pothole in his mouth as he howled before disappearing. All I could see were the soles of his feet, like unpeeled potatoes, spinning on the sand.

I was stunned. After all he had brought patrons to this 'restaurant'— how could he talk to him in that way. The proprietor's light coloured skin gave him licence to malign.
We sat down in the Jerk Centre – I no longer felt hungry – I felt confused. What justified someone being treated in that manner. Our 'tour-guide' was not causing a disturbance, in fact he was behaving in a courteous manner and yet, because he must have been a homeless person (for want of a better word), it was treated with utter disdain as though he was a leper! I found the owner's behaviour contemptuous and it made me wonder out of the two, who was the better class – who exhibited a coveted behaviour?

We were in a gazebo type construction, and it was time to order. When it arrived and I tasted the jerk chicken, I couldn't understand why the food did not taste as good as I had expected when Jamaicans were renowned for their tasty cooking.. The food wasn't appetising so I left most of it. I had been affected by the owner's behaviour. We looked at our watches and realised that it would soon be 12 noon, and the Sumfest would be soon be starting. We decided to see what it was like. When we went to the gate there was a sign: Entrance fee JA800. We were in two minds, but after conversion the entrance fee wasn't that expensive. We decided to go in, after all if there were musicians on stage it would be worth it.

The Sumfest was actually a bar that provided music and access to 'a beach'. They had cleverly instituted the 'm' for 'n' to catch people out and to lead them to think exactly how I did, that there would be a live show. It didn't matter though, we were close to the hotel so we decided to stay and look around.

There was body painting on the "Green Stripe" Girls who were exotically dressed. They were being prepared to advertise Green Stripe Soda by having the logo airbrushed onto their skin. Onlookers were mesmerised by the body curves, the colour, the vibrancy and the provocative way the Green Stripe girls told their story through dance – the performing art.

Even the structure of the Gazebo, under which the 'artists' were housed, was creative. Sticks held together with long nails, strategically placed to create an authentic shelter.

I couldn't help feeling that Jamaica was an island of artists. I could see the colours of the flag everywhere – in the green of the hills, in the gold of the sand and in the black of the skin. I longed to be a part of the artistry and the Jamaican identity notwithstanding my unfamiliarity with it. I looked at the women, admiring their vitality and nonchalance. I wanted them to recognise me as one of them and smile but it didn't happen. So I savoured the flavour of the island and watched the artist transform a woman's skin into a canvas and paint uninhibited. Nothing and no-one was ordinary! The need to feed their children and their family drove them to be innovative, whether it meant being creative with their bodies or creative with their minds. It was inspiring sitting and watching—it gave me an opportunity to reflect on my Britishness.

The part of me felt that I had a right to set the standard, but by what yardstick? Watching the Jamaican women tantalise the men forced me to assess what I had I common with them. British people had been taught to conform, to be reserved, and to be composed. It was difficult, therefore, to identify with these black matriarchs who survived by being totally liberated, expressive and uninhibited if it gave them what they wanted. For me, Jamaican women did not seem afraid of anything – they seemed bold and fearless and damned any consequences of their behaviour.

I admired their crudity and felt compelled to interpret it into an art form to give it credence and value. I felt empowered to take from both cultures, aspects which were positive. The combination of the two cultures was enriching and I felt honoured to be in a position to command a facet of either.

I found myself analysing what aspect of the Jamaican woman I would like to develop and played with the idea in my head for a while. I decided it was not being afraid. I had been brought up fearful – to watch what I say, watch what I do, to be careful of how my behaviour affected others, and to be aware of how my image was perceived by others – the internalisation of fearful messages was consistent. I did not admire the total abandonment of self-respect that I witnessed in certain situations, but I did respect the creative energy used in order to earn a living. To me, poverty was disguised in sun soaked bodies, brandishing beautiful black skin wrapped tightly around strong structures crystallised with sea water and softened with natural aloe vera.

I enjoyed watching them hustle and felt that hustling, should be given credibility and perceived as a legitimate way to earn a living.

After sitting there for a few hours observing the various activities and personalities, we noticed some Chinese-Jamaicans—Jamaicans who looked Chinese but who didn't speak Chinese and had never been to China. It was bewildering overhearing them speak with a Jamaican dialect. "Out of many one people" came to mind.

We decided that it was time to have something substantive to eat, and ordered our respective meals. Coconut shrimp; snapper; fajitas, rice and peas and vegetables came presented with cocktail glasses filled to the brim with a creamy substance, decorated with cherries, umbrellas and straws. This was our first full day, and as we indulged the delicacies until night fell upon us. Elated by the experience, satisfied with the food, it was time to go home—English time was taking its toll. The hotel was a welcome building where we all entered and dispersed into our own categories and into our own space. I put Lavender on my skin, bergamot, insect repellent, skin-so-soft in an effort to deter any insect from biting me during the night. The air conditioner breathed its fresh air into the room, and I fell asleep.

Chinese-Jamaican Connection

On the third day into the retreat, I woke up with two mosquito bites. They had become large water bubbles—one on my shin the other on my ankle. I pricked one of the bubbles and cold fluid oozed out and formed a shiny yellow track down my leg onto my ankle. I was angry at the ineffectiveness of the repellents. I surmised I must have got bitten when the electricity got cut off and the air conditioners were not working.

I had called a Chinese-Jamaican artist friend of mine, Maylien Kim6 whom I had met through the Caribbean Artists' Alliance, a non-profit organization operated by the National Cultural Committee which focused on building a strong network of the visual artists from the Caribbean. I had maintained contact over the years with Maylien Kim via email and greeting cards. I was relieved that she agreed to come to see me and share with me her perspective on Chinese culture in Jamaica. It was liberating to see Maylien Kim recant and acknowledge her ancestry, something she had no reason to do before. In fact, she hadn't even considered herself Chinese. She was first and foremost a Jamaican. She didn't speak Chinese and had never been taught it. It was her grandfather was born in China and migrated to the islands as teenager. Her grandmother was born on one of the other islands and had come to Jamaica when she was 17. Maylien Kim had never been to China and had no inclination to visit there. May-Lien's story took several hours and by mid-day we had started to feel a bit peckish. We found a Chinese restaurant near the town centre and decided that in keeping with the Chinese essence of the morning, we would to dine there.

The owner spoke Chinese and it was interesting to listen to him interact with a fellow colleague in his native tongue. The waiter, was a black Jamaican who seemed to be standing in as a manager as well, because was shouting at a young girl to get the menu. I saw her cut her eye after him, toss her head as she went through a double door. He apologised for her slowness as if to justify his behaviour, and served us in a docile manner. He said there was waterfall out back but we didn't feel like moving. The food took a long time in coming and when it finally arrived we all agreed that it was not the best we had tasted. We finished it nonetheless, said our goodbyes to Maylien-Kim, and walked towards the taxi stand. I noticed a Jerk Prawn shop across the road and knew intuitively that was where I wanted to go for my meals from then on.

The notion I had of Jamaica was too idealistic. For some reason, I felt that every one in Jamaica was an excellent cook and therefore every piece of food would 'taste sweet'. I gave no room for error or lack of expertise, it was no wonder I was disappointed.

I engaged my thoughts once again on the 0,1 Space & Identity project. My focus had become muffled leaving my subconscious to interpret my surroundings. My aim to identify with Jamaica and Jamaicans, and immerse myself in their culture was becoming distorted again, I needed to get back on track.

Venturing to Jamaica this time around, I was conscious to negate the superficial prejudices and expectations I had held on my previous visit, however I noticed that the prejudices kept repeating themselves. Something inherent in my nature was making distinctions and comparisons.

I thought I had evolved and had educated myself over the years, but I was still conscious how the differences between the British culture and the Jamaican culture either made me feel accepted or estranged, exhilarated or passive, first or second class.

We went back to the hotel and the plan for the following day was to visit the Studio of Performing Arts in Kingston.

The trip to Kingston was educational as well as entertaining. The taxi driver gave us a synopsis of the culture. He introduced me to the Ludo Game (sometimes called "Ludi"), which, along with French dominoes "…is one of the national games.." he said. The taxi driver told me how he loved playing French domino". I had never heard of 'French' dominoes and so asked him what it was. He took great pride in elaborating: " yu pose de smallest double blank, h'an den yu play at four corner – when yu at de four corner, h' if yu don't have a double yu pass and dat is ten yu are goin' get because yu are scoring. H'eny time yu don't find a double when it is yuh turn, yu get a ten.

Who has the most ten lose because dem add up the score. If yu find a double every time it comes to yu, yu alright". I could tell from his description that he had a passion for the game.

I noticed while we were driving, that Ludo boards, were displayed as an art form, hung conspicuously on rusty nails embedded into cracking wood which had a dual function – to help facilitate the stability of the structure. The Ludo boards were going for around JA$2,000 for a decent size—original art and I was sorry, on reflection, that I hadn't bought one.

Some were painted with acrylic paint while others were painted in oils in shades of blue, yellow, purple red and green, hung on a wall along with other paintings.

The taxi driver told us that the game was usually played when some-one had died during the 9 nights between death and the funeral – 'nigh-night'. It was at this time a man would "run down a table and a dice to get a play".

As we car sped down the winding road, we passed a hill of red baux-ite, a valuable commodity in Jamaica. The driver informed us that the bauxite was for aluminium, cars and pots and that he was disap-pointed with the amount of bauxite was being transported out of the country along with other natural minerals.

We drove through a long winding road, arched with trees which formed a tunnel. It was Fern Gully, renowned for getting flooded out when heavy rains fell. I saw a sign saying "Monique" as we passed which must have been another town. "There are lots of churches" I remarked to the driver. "... plenty churches", the driver said "..de pasta try fe crape up de people dem money. De pasta suppose fe drive one of de bess of de bess cyaar, h'an yu will see dem a drive rown in dem Mercedes Benz.

Dem have one pasta call Barronte who a drive de sed cyaar. But me feel seh, fram yu a deal wid de word a Gad, yu is not suppose fe deal with politic an' gun. Yet Pasta Barronte will conduct him service wid him knife h'an gun inna him waist on a Sunday marnin! Big-big gen-eral h'election and h'eny likkle crime yu wi see dem call or go fe see Pasta Barronte!"

I observed his fervour and disgust at the hypocrisy he had noticed in some of the churches.

As we approached Spanish Town, he showed us where they were

building Angel's Plaza. As we sped past I noticed what looked liked like quite a few demolished or abandoned buildings. I wondered what it would take to regenerate this part of the island that seemed to exist without enthusiasm or momentum.

It wasn't long after leaving Spanish Town that we arrived at The Studio College of the Performing Arts. Her sign prominently carved on a plaque and displayed on the corner of Riders Drive. A guard prevented us from going in at first, but on making a short call to the Head of the College, we were allowed entry. The college was very big and the grounds expansive.

We were directed to a cafeteria as we had arrived a little early and decided to go to get something to eat. Upstairs from the cafeteria, children of all races and ages were learning dance to the sound of the drum, showing a grace, artistry and brilliance of soaring eagles.

The Head called us and welcomed us into her office. She had a regal quality about her. Her refined features captivated in her fair skin. Her silver hair swooped backwards into an elegant French roll, exhibiting, among the bronze models around her, a petite frame. She sat behind what looked like a large oak desk, with a Chinese lady to her right. Her presence gave our project significance. All of us seated ourselves around the room, which was filled with the creative output of her students. She told us about the school and shared its achievements with us, and we shared the object of our visit with her. We were given an in depth tour of the College and was able to observe students being trained professionally. The techniques used in the classes were inspiring and we left feeling that visit had been beneficial.

Nightfall came quickly, and we decided to head on back to Ocho Rios which was a four hour journey. It had started raining. Fern Gully had a reputation of flooding. There were rumours that the banks might overflow. If that happened we would not be allowed to cross the bridge. We stopped at the petrol station so that the driver could fill up.

I got out and bought a drink and some peppermint drops. There were a couple of men leaning up against a broken fence who were staring. I felt that they were staring at me. Maybe they weren't. Maybe I was feeling self-conscious. Regardless of reality, I felt obsequious. I returned to the car. The driver asked if we wanted some hot bread, I immediately forgot on my reservations – food was a stimulating alternative, so he stopped outside a Bread Shop in Spanish Town where he boasted: 'dem sell de best bread in here.. h'eny time me buy one of dese bread and tek it home to my wife, she love me all night". We smiled. He returned with a hot Hardo Bread for each of us and one small one for himself – his 'wife'.

The return journey was a bit more scary because it was dark and it was raining.

The car swerved around the bends through Fern Gully. I noticed a dread emerging from the what there was of sidewalk. He looked like a prophet with his stick and his white hat. He had a regal quality and his image stuck in my consciousness for a while.

The night was black, and apart from the sparks of light that came from flying insects and a sparse amount of stars, the evening was devoid of light. We drove the remainder of the journey home in silence. I was tired and I looked forward to returning to my air-conditioned room. We stopped outside the hotel and paid the driver. Exhausted I proceed towards the hotel foyer only to see people gathered around by the pool:"Sorry maaam, d'ere is no h'electricity h'egen," explained one of the maids.

When I went into the room, the atmosphere was cloggy and warm. I imagined the presence of the mosquitoes basking in the moist hot air waiting for their victims. I opened the patio door but there was no air coming through—instead the air was heavy. It was noisy out-side. I could hear raised voices asking when there would be electric-ity. The electricity affected the phones, affected the water (so no shower); it affected the television, the light and of course the air-conditioning. The darkness of night had followed me into my room and hovered like a shroud over my head as I lay down fidgeting un-comfortably. The giggling, screaming, high-pitched voices that I could hear outside were annoying me. Inside, my imagination running wild - a foray of blood-deprived mosquitoes were waiting for me to sleep. The prospect of this happening forced me to get me to join the group outside.

After about two hours (11 at night) the electricity came on again. Unsettled, I returned to my room.

'Private' Beach

The last few days were spent on a private beach. I had been told by the hotel that they had a private beach and they directed me to where it was. When I got there, I saw a stretch of sand. No deckchairs in fact, nowhere to sit down. I felt cheated. There was a black man who looked younger than his years sitting on the corner. I asked him about the seating and he said that the deckchairs belong to the villa he was looking after but that Magnolia Gardens were con-stantly sending people down to the beach when they didn't have the facilities to accommodate them. He told me that he would take me to a 'special place' were no tourists were allowed to go but I must be there by 5:00 in the morning. I was excited and didn't say a word to anyone. It was my secret.

I should have been scared to walk early hours of the morning with a complete stranger, but I wasn't. That is why I couldn't understand the category of a tourist. A tourist would never have felt comfortable walking with a stranger through wide empty fields in Jamaica. I am not suggesting that I would have walked off with anyone, but by and large, I felt safe with my Jamaican brethren. I sensed this man who had introduced himself as Clinton was safe. He was my Jamaican brother.

I set my alarm clock and bright and early the following morning I met him as agreed. He was standing by the villa. A black face overshadowed by a red cap. He wore a white t-shirt and brightly coloured shorts. He was ready to take me on an excursion.

As I walked, I had adopted the fearlessness of my Jamaican pioneers even though I wondered where he was taking me. I could see the edge of the sea slip around a corner and out of sight. I trusted his knowledge of the island and followed him climbing over a wooden contraption that had been built in the middle of the sand. My agility was put to task as I. too, looked younger than my years!

We continued towards the part of the beach that disappeared into the sea. Clinton veered towards the right into some bushes up a hill. I hadn't told anyone where I was going, it was early in the morning, there was no-one about, so it was just "me and God" as they say. He took me through a gate that said "No trespassas – all trespassas will be prosecooted". Ignoring the warning and my concerns, he continued confidently passed the gate into an open field and I with him. I couldn't turn back now.

As I looked back, we seemed to have walked a mile at least. He was stern, not at all lascivious – his intentions were honourable. He instructed me to look where I was walking because cow dung had been dropped strategically along the path we were deemed to walk on.. I hopped and skipped over each cracked mound until we reached another gate.

I scrambled down a hill trying to grip the potholes with my feet while he descended with such grandeur. My loose fitting sandals proffered no support. As we emerged into an open space, I realised that we had walked around the part of the land that had disappeared around the corner into the horizon. I could hear water gushing but couldn't see where it was coming from. I passed several streams that came from within a rock and formed little rivers.

I continued walking, passing caves that had been forced into alcoves with the force of the sea water. I stepped timidly inside one of them and saw a mishmash of bottles, broken glass and seaweed. Supposing I found a little pot of gold or something else just as valuable, but instead I recalled a movie that had snakes and spiders so I reversed quickly and continued to follow my leader. As I walked the gushing sound was getting louder. We turned one last corner and I saw a large tree over hanging a waterfall, a boy was sitting on the branch. Children were diving in the water equipped with nozzles, catching fish. It was the locals' Dunns River Falls.

I felt privileged to have been shown this 'private haven'. "Touriss cyaan come 'ere—a fe we beach dis!" he gloated. It was at this point I felt at one with my fellow Jamaicans. He had led me to a place were tourists were not allowed to go. I felt accepted.

I sat among the men and the boys feeling unthreatened and uninhibited. These were my people! We had so much more in common than the colour of our skin. We had a style, an essence and a language that unified us.

A dread was hanging up garments and other things on the trees. This was his 'shop'. I wondered how, if this area was private and untainted by tourists, who could he be selling his wares to? I surmised that maybe locals bought stuff from him. I didn't stay long but returned with my escort and decided that I would visit the private beach again the next day, this time unescorted. My obsession not to share my experience increased. This place was privileged and I had suddenly become possessive of that space that only belonged to 'our' people.

Service with Dignity

I woke up early the next day, and crept out of the hotel before 5.00 am. I wanted to take some photographs of daybreak and dictate my experience on tape. I wanted to leave the hotel before anyone woke up. I took my towel, my pencils and sketch pad and repeated the steps of the day before. My heart was thumping as I approached the "no entry sign". I had a funny feeling that some words were missing like "trespassers shall be shot" but I followed with the steps of my ancestors, confident and strong. I remembered the cow dung and walked strategically around it.

I found the beach, and even at that early hour, loving couples were wading in the water and children were bathing in the sea. I decided to sit on a rock, and close my eyes for a while to reflect. I started to internalise images to captivate on canvas later. This private beach gave me "breathing space!". I intended to inhale the culture, the space and the environment in a spirit of consciousness.

It was beautiful being in a place that was quiet; where the white sand was puckered only by footprints. All that could be heard was the gushing of the waterfall and the sound of bodies challenging the waves. It was easy to manage my silence and moment of introspection. I looked out into the sea and wondered how far it was to the horizon.

I took this moment to reflect on where I was and how I felt in the space – this supposedly 'foreign' space. For a moment I felt at home – at ease – at peace. I had transported that aspect of my parent's culture that made me feel a part of Jamaica with me, and embraced the notion for a while.

I must have drifted off into a light sleep. A woman was sitting not too far from me eating fruit when my eyes opened. She then got up and walk towards the falls. She jumped into the imitation whirlpool, her sarong lifting with the impact. I stood up and watched her swim around. Her hair got wet but "no problem, mon". She did not seem worried about her hairstyle because she was a natural woman in natural surroundings.

Time went by quickly. The "Nyah Binghi" dread returned to his spot and started setting up shop. A black cavern widened as he smiled and I wondered why it was, so many men I had come into contact with on the beach, were void of teeth. He asked if I wanted some fish and some dumplin'. Did I? Yes I would love some.. He then asked me if I wanted some mangoes and melon. He was offering different things but I didn't see anything thing coming out of his bag. He did not have the items with him, but if I wanted them, he would have to go "faaaaar fe get dem".

It soon became clear that this was how me made his living, by offering a service. This service, instead of begging, gave him dignity. He was able to sustain himself through creativity and resourcefulness. To be honest, the fruit would have been nice if he had it with him, but the thought of him having to go so faaaaar to get it, diluted my enthusiasm. I didn't have transport so I couldn't go and buy any and even if I could, I wouldn't know where to go. He had made me feel hungry with his tempting albeit absent, menu, so I decided to go back to the hotel and return to 'my' private beach later on. It would soon be time for breakfast anyway.

We ate breakfast and I was asked where I had been. I had been missed. I had had a phone call and they realised I wasn't in my room. But the private beach was my secret. I didn't want divulge anything, so I just told them about the hotel beach which had been illegally assumed to encourage tourists to stay at their hotel.

The hotel had been boasting about their 'private beach' and I had decided to investigate the validity of their claim, but on getting there, found it was nothing but a stretch of sand. I decided to show them the hotel beach and keep the other beach to myself.

I was like a school girl with a special secret. I couldn't wait to finish my breakfast and go back there. The beach was somewhere I could stay free of charge until I was hungry. Ironically, I was experiencing the true essence of the island this way.

I took it upon myself to be obstructive. I had no intention of sharing my private island with anyone. I was going to sneak out every morning by myself, go to my private beach and get back before anyone got up for breakfast. I had my shower, got dressed and walked towards the foyer but it was as if they knew – as if they had been noticing my early morning retreats into the unknown and wanted to be a part of it. The team had convened in the foyer. I wanted to make a detour but I couldn't. At this point, I didn't feel like a team member. I didn't want to be a team member, I wanted to be on my own. I felt selfish—race, gender and background seemed to significant somehow and determined whether each or any aspect of this delineation should be allowed access to my space. I wanted to turn back but they had seen me.

"Good morning, Myrna" they greeted in unison. Where are you off to this morning?

They had caught on and were not about to allow me to go off alone without them. We were a team I had to remind myself. There was no room for isolation or alienation of any of the team members. They had been informed about the hotel's private beach and wanted to see what it was about it that captivated me. They knew I had been there before and so I was designated to take them.

My mind was scrambling information and trying to put it into a semblance of order. I didn't want to share my beach with anyone. Maybe if I showed them the 'synthetic' beach, they would be so bored with it and decide to go somewhere else so that I could then

back track later on. It was interesting how I had become so possessive of an area of land – a space which wasn't even mine to claim. But I didn't want it invaded by people of unlike mind. I had claimed it for a couple of hours a day when no-one, but a few wanderers were around. I didn't think that my behaviour was unnatural either. I had found an area where I felt comfortable, safe and at one with the elements around me. I didn't want to explain, I wanted to just be.
We all walked to the hotel beach. I could tell when they saw the barren stretch of sand that they were disappointed and could not understand my addiction to it. We saw Clinton. One of the females in the group asked where the private beach was and Clinton said he would show her. I didn't understand. Dyam faarse I thought – typical! Why couldn't she accept that this was all there was to see? I found her investigative mind irritating. And he.. he had no loyalty! I thought that the beach was not for tourists. I thought that that area was just for locals.. for Jamaicans.

These people were obviously tourists. They had their cine cameras, shorts, sandals, knapsack, while I had on my colours, my khakis and was observably Jamaican. It led me to question Clinton's perception of me. Did he take me to that beach because I was a tourist, or because I was a 'sistren? The designation was important. It mattered to me. It mattered in the sense that I wanted to know where my place was in the Jamaican mindset. Here he was, taking 'foreigners' to our private beach. His actions annulled my Jamaicanness. He had, by his desire to please and offer a service, taken them to a place reserved for 'us' — placing us all in the same category – tourists. I felt angry. I felt disappointed. I saw it as betrayal! Was nothing sacred?

I watched them walk, slowly and awkwardly along our treasured path through the meadow and down the hill – obviously unacquainted with the rough side of life and I wondered where they were going, but from the beginning of time, they have been an inquisitive race. They have always wanted to document their findings giving their presence validity and power. This was just an extension of that legacy. My 'private' beach wasn't private any more.

When we arrived, to add insult to injury, a boat load of American tourists had convened. This precious little place had become a place exploited by the locals to serve them. I watch kids swing from branches like monkeys entertaining the audience. Melon and mangoes had been sliced thinly and decoratively presented in a coconut shell which was passed around. I looked out into the sea – it was empty and vast. I wished it was land. Now I understood why the dread had set up 'shop'. I tried to regain the peace I had felt earlier by separating myself and sitting high up on the corner of a mountain, but the distraction was too severe.

As we were leaving, I checked to see what the Dread was selling. I asked him for a Ludo Board. He said he could get one, but he would need to go "clear a Browns Town fe get one". I wished I had been in a position to go to Browns Town with him as I had heard my mother mention that place when she spoke about Miss Ouida and growing up in Jamaica. I tried to visualise the place. I did not have budget for travelling expenses and so a visit to Browns Town was off the cards and the quote he gave for the Ludo Board was more than I had.

He seemed mesmerised and mentioned that he was willing to take something else instead. He had a glint in his eye. We somehow got into a conversation about tourists who came to Jamaica and what kind of services he thought tourists expected. He shared with me that the majority of women who came to Jamaica, without men were looking for 'loving'. He told me that tourists were meant to be served and he would do whatever needed to be done to serve a tourist and keep them happy – in return he would receive money or payment in kind. He was making a generalisation. There was nothing in this world he could do to keep me happy! I looked at his wide toothless mouth, his matted dreads, his dry bony foot, rough hands and bloodshot eyes and thought to myself, "im coulda have ten Ludo board likkel more, me naaaah go deh!"

The group seemed entranced by the gushing of the falls, the 'natives' scrambling around them and making a fuss, but I found the confusion disturbing.

We returned to the hotel making plans for later.

Night came down suddenly like a thick blanket over the island. The sea then became irresponsible, assuming a defiant role of its own – gushing – rising – claiming defenceless land. I became nervous, I had seen the line where the tide had ebbed and flowed and it was quite high. I wanted to feel safe. The others lagged behind so I walked back towards the villa where the beach regained her elegance as she dressed herself in twilight. Another evening completed.

Jamaica – a work of art

I decided that the next day would be spent braiding my hair. Miss Bennett said that her cousin braided hair and would do mine 'for a good price'. I had brought artificial hair with me in anticipation. She would come after breakfast. I went to bed thinking how nice it would be spending the day in the hotel having my hair braided and how transformed I would feel.

I woke up early and walked towards the beach in silence. I didn't feel like dictating the experience. I wasn't sure if I would feel the same way about it. I was prepared for anything. I took my camera and snapped flying creatures, pebbles, dislodged branches, rocks and a seashell in limbo that had been tossed in the early morning breeze. Everything on the island at that hour of the morning became a work of art and I was happy that I had made the effort.

I continued snapping at images until the film finished and I was left still wanting... The shimmering sea, the blue sky; a boy with a snorkel, a fish and a plastic bag, all possessed intrinsic character that I needed to catch on camera but had to preserve in my mind.

I wasn't as relaxed and calm as I had been. I was excited about getting my hair done on the beach. It was that time again, time for breakfast. Ackee and saltfish and dumpling. I felt hungry. I walked back to the hotel feeling energised after the early morning stroll. Breakfast was ready and so was I. I consumed it greedily. Before I finished eating, I was told that the woman who was braiding my hair was waiting for me near the villa. "She walked five miles to get here miss," announced Miss Bennett in her usual 'tannoy' tone. I felt like saying "Did I ask you anything? What has that got to do with me? She is not doing it for free!" but I kept my mouth shut. There were Jamaicans like Miss Bennett who felt the need to emphasise every milestone — all I was interested in was the end result.

After finishing my breakfast I changed my clothes and strolled down to the beach where I met the lady who was sitting on a stool she had brought with her. I wondered where I would be sitting, but decided that my rucksack would serve as a cushion for me. I was directed to where she was. I noticed the wide frame of a brightly attired woman who had her back to me. She was smoking a cigarette. Miss Bennett who had escorted me to the waterfront shouted to her cousin "Miss Diane, Miss Diane, the lady from Englan' is here for you to do her hair". I wondered why she had the inclination to expose my background. What relevance could it have other than to elicit a higher price. The woman turned around and grinned. Large 3" gold earrings were in competition with the gold teeth that spanned the whole front of her mouth and dazzled in the sunlight. The reflection dimmed her complexion and when I got closer, I wanted to tell her not to bother. She had a round face like a processed pomegranate – holey - holey. The smile was insincere and she held the scissors ajar even before the hair had come out of the bag, which looked quite menacing, especially since she had a serious scar on her cheek and one on her neck.

They have a saying : "mine who yuh let put dem han' in yuh head". Her hair betrayed her because she had one lopsided piece of wig that was much too dark for her complexion and she had forced it down over her forehead like a hat. The way she was holding the scissors, I dare not tell her not to do my hair after she had walked five miles! I had had the notion that everything people did in Jamaica was great. Great cooks, great hair stylists, bawn boasey. I didn't think I could go wrong if I let a real Jamaican braid my hair. I mean most Jamaicans have such pride in what they put their hand to. I had forgotten that the values and principles governing conscientiousness, integrity, reliability tended to be attributes applied to 'indigenous old school', and that with the young Jamaicans, money rules principles and governs the motivation when it came to tourists.

She pulled at each strand of my hair wrenching it with the braid fearlessly and aggressively. I was holding both sides of my face in pain. I told her I wanted fine braids and I even showed her a picture of how I wanted it, and yet I could see her crape up thick pieces of synthetic hair, grip a similar amount of my hair and combine the two. I knew that I should have followed my instincts and not allowed her "inna me head". I no longer felt Jamaican at that moment, because a fellow Jamaican would have cussed her out and told her fe go bowt her business! But at this juncture, I was a polite British woman; a British 'tooriss' who was about to be exploited by someone who had detected my vulnerability and passiveness in that situation. I let her finish, only grateful to survive the experience and I looked in the mirror. My head was 'gappy gappy' where shiny passageways formed in my scalp between each braid. I paid her US$20 for a job that took her 30 minutes. I was angry with myself for not speaking up.

"Your hair is really thin isn't it?" was the first comment I received.. I took them out that same evening and decided that I would braid it myself. I still had some hair left and that is what I did, and felt totally transformed as a result.

The last few days were not far different those ensuing. I wilfully embraced the people, the culture and in doing so, found fulfilment in understanding the motivation, the language and passion behind each Jamaican I came into contact with. In summary, Jamaica is a beautiful island. The treasures found in each person I came into contact with was inspiring. Had I detached myself from my mother's denigration of the language, I may well have appreciated them much more. I have grown to understand that Jamaicans are driven by the desire to rise above obstacles and to acquire a lifestyle they can feel proud of. Stepping outside and viewing from the perspective of a tourist, Jamaicans readily greet and accept with the ultimate intention to serve in anyway they can, regardless of background and heritage.

'Foreigners' who visit Jamaica are treated with dignity and they command the same in return. Conversely, even though Great Britain has accepted immigrants into her country for various reasons over the years, foreigners are feared and as a result, sense disparity in the treatment they receive.

For me, that is the other side of tourism, the side 'tourists' don't see because they are too busy having a good time being served in a variety of ways. Jamaica has naturally evolved over the years and has honed in on a much-needed market of 'personal service'. Personal service is what people crave, and why year after year, tourists re-visit. The concept of personal service in Britain, however, has been, for the most part, replaced by technology and machines so that foreigners tend not to feel as welcome.

Yes, I have felt alienated by being called a tourist in Jamaica, and alienated by being defined as an immigrant in Britain, but I have inherited the right to be among both Jamaica's "many one people" and Britain's melting pot. I have decided that a dual heritage (British-Jamaican) and the dual language (British-Creole) have rich advantages and I am proud to be a part of both!

SPACE & IDENTITY

By Myrna Loy   November 2003©

My space. My identity
Creating space for my identity..
But what is my identity
Within this space?
My parents are Jamaican,
They migrated to Great Britain,
And adopted a culture
Which was not their own.
Then I was born in Britain
And had a British education,
but then married a Jamaican
and merged two cultures into one.

I learned the Jamaican custom
I cook Rice 'n' peas and chicken,
A British-born Jamaican
That is what I am!
But in Jamaica they call me 'foreign'
And an immigrant in Britain
So pray tell me something
Where do I belong?
I have been acknowledging an ancestry
Which really doesn't belong to me,
Because Britain is where I was born
And therefore is my home.

The End

Myrna Loy, Dip C (Inst. NH), is a product and living example of how the arts facilitated her growth & development. When Loy was going through a tumultuous time, she would paint from her imagination, which tended to have a futuristic quality, but it is where she found solace.

Myrna is the author of Lover's Rock – More than a Dance Floor (explaining the healing and hurting aspect of the era) Spirit of Queens (Spirit-led Poetry), Poetry's Promise (which is an intimate insight into the author's personal life); Poetry's Teacher (which shares her practical life experiences) and The Other Side of Tourism (which highlights the author's prejudices and conflict as a Black Brit) examining her Jamaican roots. This novelette was endorsed by Lord Ouseley (House of Lords), Dianne Abbot (House of Commons) and Patricia Lashley (Momentum Arts, Cambridge) who wrote an extensive review on The Other Side of Tourism.

Loy is currently a social influencer under the name, 'Blackbright News' on YouTube, and uses her life experiences, knowledge and empathy to inform her subscribers.

Loy is the Publisher and Managing Editor of Blackbright News, which was the first of its kind that serves people of colour from a political and social context. Issues of Black-Bright News, can located at www.issuu.com/blackbrightnews, and can be downloaded for free.

Loy is also a qualified Counsellor and Teacher of Adult Literacy. As an extension of her teaching, Loy offers 'counselling' on YouTube, under the banner of Dark Shades Counselling.

Born in London, Loy moved to the United States, where she was fortunate enough to land herself a position with the United Nations. Loy became the Senior Assistant to the Chief of Staffing, and also served on the Office of Human Resources Advisory Panel. Loy also worked for the Assistant Secretary General to the United Nations Development Fund (UNDP), for a short while after returning from UNAVEM II Peacekeeping mission in Luanda (Angola, where she served as a Personnel Officer, Logistics Officer and sat on the Board of Enquiry for 11 months. Loy was also a member of the UNDP Editorial Board to the United Nations.

UK, America, Jamaica and Africa's life lessons have prepared Myrna for where she is today, honing in on every aspect she has learned by being a Project Manager, a UN diplomat, Administrator, writer, poet and a painter to create, produce, market and publish and re-establish herself in the realm of the arts and social influencing.

Myrna Loy (aka Lady Loy)'s past-time on the last Friday of the month, is an honorary radio DJ/Presentor for Loversrock Radio (www.loversrockradio.com) and has been presenting on radio since 2008.

Printed in Great Britain
by Amazon

56231858R00079